THE SOCIAL SCIENCES AND AFRICA'S FUTURE

30th Anniversary Essay Competition Winners

Knowledge Rajohane Matshedisho
Claude Abé
Mildred Kiconco Barya
Esther Van Heerden
Ingrid Palmary

COUNCIL FOR THE DEVELOPMENT OF
SOCIAL SCIENCE RESEARCH IN AFRICA

CODESRIA

ISBN: 2-86978-170-9   ISBN-13: 978-2-86978-170-2

Typesetting: Hadijatou Sy

Cover Design: Ibrahima Fofana

Printed by Lightning Source

The Council for the Development of Social Science Research in Africa
(CODESRIA) is an independent organisation whose principal objectives are
facilitating research, promoting research-based publishing and creating multiple
forums geared towards the exchange of views and information among African
researchers. It challenges the fragmentation of research through the creation of
thematic research networks that cut across linguistic and regional boundaries.

CODESRIA would like to express its gratitude to African Governments, the
Swedish Development Co-operation Agency (SIDA/SAREC), the International
Development Research Centre (IDRC), OXFAM GB/I, the MacArthur
Foundation, the Carnegie Corporation, the Norwegian Ministry of Foreign Affairs,
the Danish Agency for International Development (DANIDA), the French
Ministry of Cooperation, the Ford Foundation, the United Nations Development
Programme (UNDP), the Rockefeller Foundation, the Prince Claus Fund and
the Government of Senegal for support of its research, publication and training
activities.

Contents

Notes on Contributors

Knowledge R Matshedisho is a PhD candidate in the Department of Sociology at the University of Cape Town, where he has also lectured for some years. He is currently lecturer in Sociology at the University of the Witwatersrand, South Africa.

Claude Abé is currently working on a dissertation in Sociology. He holds a doctorate in information and communication sciences from Université de Paris, and an MPhil in Sociology and is a lecturer at the Université catholique d'Afrique centrale in Yaoundé, Cameroon. Other than engaging the epistemology of social sciences in Africa, he also works on social communication and urban social dynamics and African politics.

Mildred Kiconco Barya is a writer, poet and human resource consultant. She is the author several poems, short stories and articles published in magazines, newspapers, and anthologies in Africa, Europe and the United States. Among these include *Men, Love Chocolates But They Don't Say*, a collection of poetry; *Call me a Panda*, a children's novel with Fountain Publishers; and 'Effigy Child', a short story for the Commonwealth Broadcasting Association, and Raindrops, an anthology of short stories published by FEMRITE, Uganda.

Ingrid Palmary is a former senior researcher at the Centre for the Study of Violence and Reconciliation and is currently employed at the University of the Witwatersrand in the Forced Migration Studies Programme. She has published in the areas of gender and forced migration, feminist activism, the intersections of 'race' and gender in armed conflict, domestic violence and research methods for the social sciences.

Esther van Heerden is currently writing-up a doctorate in Social Anthropology at the University of Cape Town. She graduated from the universities of Stellenbosch (BA International Studies) and Cape Town (MA in Social Anthropology) both in South Africa. As an exchange student at Uppsala, Sweden, she assisted on a research project about HIV transmission and infant feeding. Her research focuses on the spatial and temporal dimensions of contemporary South African arts festivals.

Reflections from the Future

Is it enough to merely claim that young people are our future, to make the future happen? Much more than just words, the future needs to be supported in an effective and sustainable way so that it can happen. Today, Africa's youth are facing multiple constraints, brought about by an unfavourable historical context, in a much more acute way than was the case for the previous generation. Indeed, the current difficulties afflicting the continent are affecting young people even harder, and they do not seem to see any end to it. Even worse, the young are the victims of a collective stigmatisation, which considers them more as a threatening category than as a group to bank on for the future. Some think they are a dangerously perverted group, while others see them as a group messed up by a consumerist culture; in short, Africa's youth are accused of being the root of all evil. They are unfairly blamed for all the problems, and the so-called apathy they demonstrate is a source of concern, and also a source of Afro-pessimism. It is said that the younger generation is less committed than the previous generation, and is therefore less involved in major African issues. The African younger generation is said to be desperately silent. Can African youth be a source of future prosperity for the continent, as it is often asked, with obvious concern? Should we give up hope about the new generation when the young, however, are too often criticized, and seldom listened to? The so-called silence of the younger generation may be explained by the deafness of the older generations. It is therefore high time that we listened to young African academics, so that they can discuss and define their own projects for the future. It has been acknowledged that no conscious act aimed at improving human life can be successful, if it is not guided by knowledge. In so doing, the youngest researchers should accept their responsibility: they should produce knowledge and put it at the disposal of African populations. Aware of the need to promote an exchange of ideas and experiences between young Africans, CODESRIA has decided to create a collection for them entitled *Interventions*, in the framework of a strategic initiative aimed at promoting young researchers.

Through the publication of essays written by young scholars, this initiative is aimed at promoting an open debate among Africa's youth about African issues. We hope that these essays will be an opportunity for young people to get involved in public and/or academic debates about the future of the continent. This publication is conceived of as a collective campaign with the mission of examining the various developmental aspects of African societies to lead to increased self-awareness about our common future. The texts in this volume have been selected after an essay competition organised for CODESRIA's thirtieth anniversary. Researchers under the age of thirty were invited to reflect on the complex relationship between the input of social sciences and the building of an African future. Indeed, one of the major contemporary issues to be considered in a future-oriented perspective is the role of scientific knowledge in improving the life of individuals. This narrow link between scientific practice and the advancement of societies is a real challenge for the African scientific community, within which young people will be able to play a significant role. The five texts published may be individual responses of young researchers, but they are above all a reflection of a collective path, that of the African youth who have not given up the fight, and who are making themselves heard through a self-confident and demanding reflection, already infused with wisdom. The young authors, who criticize the past and are unsatisfied with the present, are attempting to define a new way, according to the spirit and orientation that each of them would like to give to scientific practice, the status of the researcher and also to the African historical perspective. One can feel that a dialogue is being created through all of this, a form of unity in the targeted objective. To some, these theses will sound a bit naïve, ingenuous, or naïvely optimistic. But no one can accuse these young authors of not being sincere and showing commitment; no one can ignore this obvious desire to play their role as researchers, and put this new form of science at the disposal of Africans. By helping to explain how African societies of today and yesterday work, these young authors will help build an enlightened future.

We hope that these essays will motivate young researchers to write, express themselves and make this collection serve as an echo for words for the future that Africa is so lacking. Along with wise and reasonable advice, they will also receive support from their elders in their effort to build a brighter future for Africa. For this initiative to be successful, the essays in this collection must be read, criticized and commented upon.

Happy reading!

Adebayo Olukoshi   Jean-Bernard Ouédraogo
Executive Secretary   Head Training, Grants & Fellowships
CODESRIA   CODESRIA

Reinterpreting and Reconstructing Africa: The Challenge for Social Science Scholarship

Knowledge Rajohane Matshedisho

Introduction

I argue that social sciences are relevant for the reconstruction and reinterpretation of Africa. My argument is based on four premises. The first one is that the social sciences as conceptualised in the West and introduced into Africa have denied the interpretation of Africa as a civilised continent and hence justified slavery and colonialism. The second premise is that social sciences have been used across Africa in popular and literary struggles against the colonisation of African countries. The third premise is that in post-independence Africa, social sciences can and should be used in the reconstruction of Africa. The final premise is that in the process of reconstruction and reinterpretation of Africa, it is critical that there is a multidisciplinary approach both within the social sciences and between the social sciences, and natural science, business science, and information and communications technology.

The first part of my essay is an analysis of the colonial discourse in Africa and the colonial understanding of civil society. The second part describes the role of the social sciences in popular struggles against colonialism in Africa. The third part argues for a greater need of the social sciences in post-colonial Africa than it now seems to be accepted. The final part advocates a multidisciplinary approach in studies and research in the social sciences.

Civil society, colonisation and the Social sciences in Africa

In his provocative analysis in *Citizen and Subject*, Mamdani (1996) argues that the concept of civil society in Africa developed differently to that of Europe. The construction of the concept and its application in Africa was imbued with the colonial 'othering' racial discourse. The concept of civil society was used to differentiate the 'civilised' from the 'uncivilised'—that is, the Europeans from the indigenous Africans. Civil society was therefore exclusionary and discriminatory. It was a socio-economic, political, aesthetic and scholarly space or terrain exclusively reserved for Europeans and expressly barred to indigenous African 'subjects'. He observes, 'the history of civil society in colonial Africa is laced with racism. That is, as it were, its original sin, for civil society was first and foremost the society of colons. Also, it was primarily a creation of the colonial state' (Mamdani 1996:19). Mamdani uses this observation to give an understanding of the development and structure of the state in Africa. I, however, use his observation to argue that the representation and 'understanding' of Africa in Western scholarship in the social sciences has been equally racist and Eurocentric.

The concept of civil society as applied in Africa by colonists encapsulated the misrepresentation and suppression of African art, music, religion, education, history, philosophy, languages,

ideologies, economies and political life. I think essentialism
is the cardinal philosophical flaw underlying the social sciences
as introduced in Africa in trying to 'understand' social life
and social formations among Africans. The word 'African' does
not just carry a continental reference, but rather implicitly
connotes some commonality and essence. In effect 'African'
is that which has certain distinguishable properties without
which it can never be African, while other properties in African
may be considered incidental. Such thinking still persists today
and I disagree with it. I think the notion of the 'essence' in
Africa is at the philosophical root of the misrepresentation of
Africa in the social sciences scholarship. It is the 'essence' of
the 'civilised' and the 'uncivilised'. The 'essence' of and what
counts as the social sciences scholarship and what is rejected
as not the social sciences scholarship.

Early analysis of African societies utilising European
conceptual tools was underpinned by scientific racism. 'During
the era of colonial rule the pressure of European scientific
racism increased both in intensity and sophistication. Firmly
in control on the ground, European scientists could examine
at leisure: testing mine workers in South Africa, studying the
effects of malnutrition in Kenya, observing epidemics on the
Gold Coast or analysing tribal taboos in Rhodesia' (July
1989:203). The discourse was characterised by the application
of Western anthropological categories of social formations and
the human processes within those formations. With these
conceptual tools the indigenous African people's physical
appearance, cuisine, religions, architecture, music, dances and
culture were compared to the Western anthropological grid
and they did not match. Consequently what did not match
with Europe was regarded as 'uncivilised', 'barbaric', 'savage',
'idiotic', 'bestial', and 'primitive'. All these qualifications were
synonymous with the indigenous people of Africa as opposed
to the 'civilised' Europeans. From the beginning, European

scholarship understood the genus people of Africa as the 'other', who were 'uncivilised' and had to be 'civilised'. The need to 'civilise' Africans has been a theme that ran through the colonisation process even in post-colonial Africa. However, in post-colonial Africa, the discourse has changed from that of civilisation to that of development. Western scholarship in the social sciences has shifted from civilising Africa to developing Africa.

Development theory is the late example of the problem of essentialising Africa. The idea of development as conceptualised and understood in Western social sciences scholarship is a functionalist way of thinking. Development has been understood as a linear process from prehistoric societies to modern capitalist ones. Rostow (1960) analysed the development of western societies in this linear fashion, which is termed modernisation theory. Thereupon he concluded, 'It is possible to identify all societies, in their economic dimensions as lying within five categories: the traditional society, the preconditions for take-off, the take-off, the drive to maturity and the age of high mass consumption'. Needless to say that such understanding of economic development has characterised development policy in Africa and has been predominantly used to explain underdevelopment in Africa too. Development discourse, as understood and underpinned by modernisation theory, has, since the 1950s, not only misrepresented economies in Africa and their colonial destabilisation, but also silenced the different voices within the African continent. The history and 'development' of Africa was understood within the framework of modernisation theory mediated by essentialism in what is considered essentially African and what is considered essentially European. For Africa to be 'civilised' it too had to follow the developmental pattern of Europe. 'Africans were a people who had no history, who knew nothing about their environment, had no basic technology and so on. Hence it was thought that the colonising structures already put in place could be expanded to take care of all the physical and social transformation that was needed' (Nketia 1994:7). This transformation had to happen not only in developing Africa in economic terms but also with respect to the cultural, historical, political, religious and aesthetic way of life. Africa had to be Europe. Such were the disciplines in the social sciences about Africa.

Not only has Western social science scholarship misrepresented Africa; it has disregarded African social science scholarship. Nketia observes that 'the place of African social sciences in academia has always been problematic because of a natural tendency to give pride of place to the Western experience. Thus until recently music, art, literature etc. meant western music, western art, western literature unless specifically qualified. Universities in America list courses that should be taken to satisfy the social sciences requirements such as English, literature, music, and then African literature, world music and so on' (Nketia 1994:11). Nketia (1986) also notes how African musicology had been studied through Western understandings of music and how such studies have changed in reinterpreting and restudying African musicology. Mazrui (1986) quotes a Professor of History at Oxford in 1963 who said that African history is the study of the 'unrewarding gyrations of barbarous tribes in picturesque but irrelevant corners of the globe', (Mazrui 1986:14). Similarly Mamdani (1998) observes that

> historically, African Studies developed outside Africa, not within it. It was a study of Africans, but not by Africans. The context of this development was colonialism, the Cold War and apartheid. This period shaped the organisation of social sciences studies in the Western academy... The disciplines studied the White experience as a universal, human, experi-

ence: area studied the experience of people of colour as an
ethnic experience (1998:1).

Diop (1996) also argues against the colonial displacement of
history in Africa. In particular he argues for an intellectual
development in Africa with an understanding of the African
context. His overall findings and argument are that Western
scholarship in the social sciences has suppressed the history
of civilisation in Black Africa and that there is dire need to
rediscover Africa by African scholars guided by African ideology
and culture. Social sciences, as introduced in Africa were thus
imbued with essentialism and racism.

Social sciences in post-colonial Africa

It follows from the above arguments that scholars in Africa
advocate the reinterpretation of Africa within the social
sciences and the reorganisation of analytical tools used in such
disciplines. Marks (2000) argues that there is a need to teach
social sciences in South African universities mainly for four
reasons. First, to dispel the myths created by the Western
conceptualisation of Africa; second, to reinterpret history in
Africa in a non-essentialising manner; third, to study the social
sciences in a manner that will not juxtapose the natural
sciences and social sciences in a diametrically opposed fashion,
but rather in mutually infused positions for the development
of the continent both in terms of technology and social life.
The final reason is to realise that studying Africa has
destabilised Western conceptual tools, and to call for the
reconceptualisation of both African and Western scholarship
in the social sciences.

Bates (1993) has compiled articles that dealt with the
contribution of research in Africa to social science and the
humanities. (He distinguishes between social science and the
humaniies). These articles demonstrate how the study of
African societies has made for a better understanding of Africa

by questioning Western epistemology. For example Moore (1993) focuses on the anthropological study of African studies prior to the 1960s and more recently. She shows how a reflexive study of African societies has changed the analytical tools and content of anthropology in general and in the African context. Similarly Miller (1993) begins to ask how literary studies could be understood in Africa when part of our history is an oral one, but colonialists in colonial languages write the other part. Both these authors and the others indicate the need to use the social sciences or humanities in reconstructing our past intellectually. The aim is not to come up with African social sciences, but rather to recreate the disciplines within the social sciences in a manner that dispels the myths in understanding African societies.

I think the relevance of the role of the social sciences in contemporary Africa is justified by Kwame Nkrumah's Consciencism, Mazrui's cultural integration, Masolo's modernism and scientific universalism, Bell's cross-cultural philosophy and my understanding of globalisation and higher education. Mazrui (1986) is sympathetic to Kwame Nkrumah's consciencism, which acknowledges Africa's experience with African indigenous culture, Islamic and Christian influences and the need for the synthesis of these cultures for the development of Africa. He then stretches Nkrumah's consciencism to urge the need for 'a quest for national cultural integration in every African country... a quest for cultural convergence at the continental level... a search for a developmental ideology compatible with African culture' (Mazrui 1986:34). While Mazrui makes a good case for national cultural integration and a developmental ideology, his idea of a Pan African cultural integration is problematic because it essentialises Africa and seeks to practically homogenise it. Like the colonial discourse, which sought to unearth the 'essence' of Africa, Mazrui counteracts the myths but still works within the colonial epistemology of essentialism.

I recognise the limitations of Mazrui's quest for African homogeneity when I read Bell (2002) on *Understanding of African Philosophy*. Bell states that he is a non-African. His book eliminates essentialism in understanding philosophy in Africa. While the name African philosophy might be misleading in implying the long tradition of a homogenous Africa, his analysis rejects the illusion of unanimity in understanding African societies. He acknowledges the diversity and plurality in philosophical thinking in Africa. Instead of trying to integrate these philosophical thought into an African package he argues that one-especially non-Africans-should use such diversity to understand one's own and the other's philosophy. He demonstrates that Africa has a rich multiplicity of philosophies and these philosophies can only be understood if one listens and learns from them. He also adds that non-Africans can learn more about their philosophies by understanding African philosophy. In this way, I think Bell tries to show that there can never be an 'essence' of what is African, European or Asian. Rather he shows that categories and 'essences' are blurred in everyday life and cannot be justified even in philosophical terms.

Similarly Masolo (1994) traces the debates in African philosophy and shows how they have emanated from emotivism and logocentrism, and how they were imbued with Africanism. In his introductory chapter he summarises as follows:

> the history of African philosophy is therefore the history of Africa in a special way. It is the history of Africanism in its critical expressions and articulations. This intellectual quest precedes and forms the foundation for the diversified attempts to deconstruct the old colonial sciences. History took the lead in the 1950s, followed by literature in the 1960s and

political science and sociology in the 1970s. At the base of the revolution of the 1960s of the transfer of intellectual leadership and administrative authority in general to management by Africans themselves, rests this search for new ideas and new forms of abstraction (Masolo 1994:45).

He shows how African philosophy has engaged with Western philosophy and colonial scholarship in the social sciences. He concludes that there is a need for African philosophy to step away from a defensive Africanism and to appreciate diversity within Africa and elsewhere in terms of culture, history and scholarship. He advocates a pluralistic approach to African philosophy. He says,

> there is no single philosophical tradition that was tailor made and produced like an industrial product. There is no justifiable reason, therefore, why one individual or group should try to tailor African philosophy by prescribing what ought to be its content, method of reasoning and standards of truths... So while we say yes to African personality, we ought to also say yes to technological modernism: yes to the African conscience, but also yes to universal science.

Masolo too dispels essentialism by advocating an African identity which is intellectually cognisant of universal scholarship in the social sciences. He argues that there is a need for greater philosophical work in Africa both to dispel the myths of the past and to give new meanings within and relative to other philosophies of the world.

Falola and Jennings (2002) have assembled several readings dealing with the ways in which authors have tried to use knowledge in African settings to make better sense of African scholarship in both Africa and in other parts of the world. The readings are both argumentative and reflexive in their approach to the social sciences in Africa. An interesting observation about these readings is that they are multidisciplinary and they do not essentialise Africa, but rather research Africa in reflective manner. For example, Eagleson (2002) provides an interesting historical account and reception of the Kenyan popular song 'Malaika' in America. He tries to explain not only the socio-cultural settings within which the song was popularly received, but also the technical aspect of the music and of the rendition itself, in order to give an account of the impact of an African song in a non-Kenyan setting, and how it has contributed to the understanding of the rise of folk music around the world. Such analysis not only produces knowledge from Africa, it also—as Masolo argues—encompasses universal science through which we can understand our experiences in Africa relative to other cultures within and outside Africa. Such analysis not only shows the relevance of the social sciences in Africa but also the incorporation of multidisciplinary approaches and the appreciation of cultural diversity rather than Afrocentrism, which is a mirror image of Eurocentrism.

Intellectual struggles against colonialism are important as a foundation of intellectual progress in Africa. In post-colonial Africa and the global economy there is more that needs to be done than just dispelling colonial myths. Social science scholarship has to move beyond emotivism, logocentrism and essentialism. It has to address current challenges that face Africa within the global economy of capitalism and cultural diversities. I concur with the Task Force on Education (2000) that only general education will be able to address most of the socio-cultural and developmental needs in Africa. The reinterpretation of Africa in history, literature, and the arts cannot be done in a fragmented manner or just by choice. Rather there needs to be a concerted and synergistic effort. Higher education is the primary terrain on which general education could be reconstructed to meet the challenges facing our continent. By general education, it is meant what is usually called liberal education. The negative connotation of the term liberal education is obvious. However, Masolo reminds us that our contextual needs should take account of universal science from which we can debate or challenge further. There are several reasons why higher education and why general education are at issue.

According to the Task Force on Education and Society (2000:83-84), higher education should meet goals such as:

- Satisfying the demand from students for an increasingly sophisticated and rewarding education.
- Training the people needed to run a modern society and contribute to its further advancement
- Providing a forum in which a society can examine its problem and identify appropriate solutions; and
- Offering a setting in which a society's culture and values can be studied and developed.

According to the Task Force (2000:84), general education produces a graduate who can think and write clearly, effectively, and critically, and who can communicate with precision, cogency and force. Such a student will have a critical appreciation of the ways in which we gain knowledge and understanding of our universe, of society and of ourselves. The right kind of education will ensure a broad knowledge of other cultures and other times, and enable people to make decisions based on a reference to the wider world and to the historical forces that have shaped it. Further, general education should furnish students with an understanding of and experience in thinking systematically about moral and ethical problems and enable them to achieve depth in some field of knowledge.

In the case of developing countries like Africa I would add that the higher education curriculum should be the bedrock of lifelong learning, human-centred sustainable development ideas and policy implementation programmes. I also add that general education should produce graduates with a synergistic and interdisciplinary approach to problem solving. These characteristics and the ones outlined by the Task Force are necessary for addressing the pressing problems we find in African countries. Let us take a look at some of our contemporary problems and how social sciences could be utilised as part of the skills needed for the resolution thereof.

The value of the social sciences has been debated in post-1994 South Africa. The debate has centred around the role of the social sciences in the changing South Africa and the need for career-focused programmes in higher education. The point was made in education policy frameworks such as the Education White Paper 3 – by the Department of Education (1997) – that social science graduates were not marketable compared to those in science and business. The conclusion was that universities should concentrate on marketable subjects. Scholars in the social sciences did not agree with such policy directions. Dowling (1998) argues that such arguments are simplistically utilitarian and produce no evidence to support their claims. He also states that applied ethics can solve some problems, which chemistry and engineering cannot. Nel and van der Westheizen (1998:7) argue that 'the government's rationale to marginalise ratiocinative disciplines located in the social sciences in itself denotes an even more disconcerting propensity, viz. the naïve idea that epistemological systems are primarily informed by skills and not the other way round'. Mzamane (1998) argues that cultural studies in South Africa are vital for nation building. He asserts that we need an inventory of art forms in South Africa and a curriculum for cultural studies that would take into account that a majority of South Africans have been denied training in culture and art which can 'provide the necessary liberation ethos for deprogramming, decolonisation and dealienation' (Mzamane 1998:11). On history, Lange (1998:20) states that

> historians are still the caretakers of collective memory. They have to tell stories of what people say happened, of what people felt when it happened. They have to help societies in different stages of development to come to terms with their often conflictive and contradictory identities and pasts. But historians do not only tell stories. At the same that they narrate, they explain, they look for reasons, purpose, cause.

I understand there is a popular argument against teaching social sciences, which states that higher education is producing more social science graduates than the economy can absorb. Or that social science graduates do not find jobs because the economy needs graduates who are skilled in information and communication technology, business and actuarial science, natural science, medicine and engineering. I don't deny that economic and social development requires natural and business science skills. But I think that the problem is not that the social science graduates cannot find a place in the labour market. The problem is that for centuries knowledge has been fragmented and sub-divided into science and social sciences. There was no social dimension in fields such as medicine, business, architecture, engineering and computer technology. Patients were diagnosed, given treatment and a prognosis without an understanding of social factors that might have prevented the illness or that could have enhanced recovery. Manufacturing has operated with no regard to the environment and its impact on the health of the population. Buildings have been designed with no regard to people who are suffering from physical disability or elder people who cannot access them as easily as before. Education itself has been imparted without taking into account the different levels of preparedness and cultural differences which might impact on learners. Development policies have been formulated with no regard to sustainability and human development. The widely used production value indicators, the Gross Domestic Product and Gross National Product, do not incorporate a dimension respecting the human cost of economic activities. Such gaps have therefore created a low demand for people who are skilled to fill them.

These gaps are slowly being filled, as the world is realising that we cannot create goods and services for people if we disregard their welfare in the process. General education and the continuation of the social sciences in Africa may not show positive results in the short run. However I concur with the Task Force (2002) that in the long run there will be positive results. Our present challenges in Africa demand a thorough grounding in the social sciences.

Let us take a look at South Africa. This country is referred to as a democratic miracle because of its smooth transition from apartheid to multiparty politics. Of course it is a miracle relative to the scourge of civil war and rebel movements in post-independence African countries such as Rwanda, Angola, Liberia, Burundi, Democratic Republic of Congo, Sudan and Côte d'Ivoire. However, the South African democracy is faced with some challenges in which the social sciences need to play a greater role than any other category of disciplines. Firstly there is the stark xenophobia reflected in the way foreigners from other African countries are addressed derogatorily. Such problems are understandable because South Africa grew out of a context of racism and ethnicism in which not only was there an institutionalised divide between people of different 'races', there was also a cultural divide within people of the same 'races'. The English-speaker was different from the Afrikaner. The Zulu was different from the Sotho and occupied different 'homelands'. It is therefore not surprising that in our incipient democracy South Africans stereotype African foreigners and make them feel unwanted, while being unable to stereotype white foreigners or express an opinion about them. Such a problem could be addressed by general education at various levels, particularly in higher education where diversity and plurality could be better understood in terms of their contribution to economic, social and intellectual development. Other problems that we face in South Africa are the legacy of racism, the challenge of nation building, reconciliation and promoting a human rights culture. The list is long.

The case of Amina Lawal who was sentenced to death by stoning by the Regional Court of Katsina state in Nigeria in May 2002 is another case in point. She was found guilty of adultery because she bore a baby outside marriage. A higher court later acquitted her in October 2004 after two appeals. This case was not simply about legal procedures but it was interpreted from various perspectives, so much so that I think it will remain as a historical example. Some saw Amina as a victim of poverty in which there was trial without representation. Others saw Amina as an example of the oppression of women, especially those who are black and poor. Some saw the trial as a misinterpretation of the Islamic Law and its procedures. Others saw it as a violation of human rights and the need to mobilise and campaign internationally for her release. We cannot be certain which perspective best explains the situation. However, I would suggest that different forces with different identities and perspectives have contributed towards an understanding of Amina's situation, bringing about a deeper perspective on the depth of the matter. Even though everyone called for her acquittal, the reasons were different but in synergistic and interdisciplinary fashion she was ultimately acquitted. I am not suggesting that a plurality of ideas is a quick fix for every problem. I am suggesting that while different perspectives might have essentialised Amina as a woman or black or African or Muslim or a human being with rights, the totality of these identities sparked a fruitful debate and the reconsideration of the situation from different angles. The end result was that a much more informed understanding of the situation for the courts, and for us as scholars in the social sciences. Such is the task of African countries to try and see their problems from different perspectives and reach an intellectually informed decision and practical resolutions. Unfortunately the lack of such methods of thinking and planning produced strife and civil wars in Africa.

Civil wars have been, and in some cases remain, a scourge in African countries such as Angola, Democratic Republic of Congo, Côte d'Ivoire, Rwanda, Sierra Leone, Liberia, Ethiopia and Eritrea. Different observers postulate different reasons for the wars. Some observers' causal factors are other observers' triggering factors. It is common to say that there is ethnic war in countries such as Rwanda or Angola. And that civil war in countries such as Nigeria is caused by religious conflicts between Muslims and Christians. Even in the case of conflict in South Africa just before the 1994 elections the factors were said to be between the political parties ANC and IFP, or even more bluntly, between Xhosa-speaking people and Zulu-speaking people. It is never easy to uncover the real causes as no one wants to be blamed and that there is always a multiplicity of factors. Some authors argue that civil wars in Africa are not ethnic but rather economic. Collier et al. (2000) conclude that:

1. Africa's ethnic diversity is not a cause of the recent rise in the incidences of civil wars that impacted the region. Indeed, other things being equal Africa is inherently safer than other regions because of its social diversity.

2. Before Africa can turn its ethnic diversity into an asset for preserving peace it must achieve better levels of political freedom, much higher standards of living and diversified economies.

3. To achieve economic development and hence contribute to prevention of future wars, both "appropriate" political governance (i.e. functioning democracy) and high quality institutions for economic management would be required for mitigating the possibly adverse economic consequences of social diversity' (http://www.eldis.org/static/DOC7755.htm, accessed 25 October 2003).

Even though they argue that the underlying factors are economic, they still do not explain why such conflicts take on ethnic or religious dimensions. I think that such cleavages are significant and worthy of scrutiny. It is not by historical accident that ethnicity and religion act as conduits of political strife or causal factors there of. The fragmentation of African societies by colonialism is primarily responsible for this situation. Africa is not an exception though. Northern Ireland's religious conflicts are a case in point. My contention is that such civil wars in Africa might well be due to poverty but that no matter how opulent a country may be, if there is no tolerance there would be conflict one way or the other and certain cleavages would emerge to express that conflict. In our social science scholarship, we need to change the culture of forced homogeneity. Was there ever a truly homogenous society? If there had been, then we would not have diametrical terms and connotations such as outcasts and community, rich and poor, masses and elite, government and citizens, lords and commons; or for that matter women and men. We can only change such modes of thinking through a general education, which makes the social sciences an integral part of curriculum in both schools and institutions of higher learning.

It is only through an appreciation of other cultures and critical thinking that people can learn to look beyond their own identities of ethnicity, religion and social status. In fact one's own history and identity is enriched by understanding other histories and identities.

The consequences of civil war are far reaching and one of them, which I choose as an example, is physical disability from war, trauma cases or birth defects as a result of war chemicals, war famine or lack of antenatal care due to war and displacement. Impairment is a medical condition but disability is a social condition in which people living with disabilities experience society in their everyday life. Common stereotypes about people with disabilities are documented around the world from as early as ancient Greece to contemporary industrial societies as demonstrated by Garland (1995). The depiction of people living with disabilities does not only end there. People with disabilities have also been subjected to public spectacles in forms of amusement and so depicted in some forms of art. Thomson (1996) compiled readings which demonstrate how art and aesthetics have depicted people with disabilities or different physical features. The images of difference are negative and suggestive of an inferior position that is generally occupied by people living with disabilities. Sarah Baartman is an example of how bodily difference led to her becoming a public showcase of amusement and a victim of abuse. Oliver (1990) and Oliver (1996) demonstrate the historical construction of disability and the struggles faced by people living with disabilities. Even at the personal level, people with disabilities face constraints that society imposes on them. For example, Felix Silwimba observes, 'Sexual relationships for persons with disabilities are often left out in discussions of the disabled persons' problems. The teachings and actions of society require that disabled persons repress their sexual desires... Thus when the concept of sexuality is thrown aside in planning rehabilitation of the disabled, emphasis is on teaching only the most elementary skills by which somebody who has a disability can become economically independent. Therefore, these persons remain a liability to society, are consequently excluded from the basic human need of expressing and feeling love'. Popular consciousness has been negatively shaped on this terrain by social sciences, and people with disabilities have been constructed as such and their daily experiences made difficult.

The need to deconstruct disability is relevant in Africa as it is in any part of the world for five reasons. Firstly the then Organisation of African Unity (now African Union) declared the period 2000–2009 the African Decade of Disabled Persons. Although such declarations to create awareness, they should also be used to encourage vigorous research in disability studies. Literary studies need to deconstruct texts on disability and art needs to examine the ways it has depicted difference. Secondly, some people living in Africa who experience disabilities were 'normal' before they were victims of war or trauma. It is therefore morally just that such people be enabled to live a normal social life. Thirdly, Africa has to resocialise its people into the paradigmatic shift from a medical paradigm of disability to a social one, in which the problem is no longer seen as an individual tragedy but as society which makes it difficult for people with disabilities to function in their everyday life. Fourthly, development is not about economic output only but human and environmental sustainability. If society neglects people then development is not holistic. In this case the identity and well being of people with disabilities needs to be taken into account. Finally, it is through the social sciences that a social model of disability could be achieved. The media needs to stop representing disabled people as others. The media and our institutions should be able to represent people with disabilities, and stand up for them.

People with disabilities should not be used as inferior objects of entertainment. Such ideals could be realised if we debate about the value of a human being; the rights of human beings; what counts as non-discriminatory art; and what is disability. Of course social sciences cannot work alone to bring about such ideals. Medical professionals, engineers, architects and statisticians have a critical role in aspects such as medical rehabilitation, assistive technology design, and building design for access and demographics for policy interventions.

I also think that at the heart of the problems facing Africa is the leadership crisis-dictators who appoint themselves as life presidents, or gerrymander election processes and suppress opposition, and squander public funds when the general populace lives in squalor. It is pure corruption that hinders even the slight chances of development and moral regeneration in Africa. No matter how much funding a country receives, if the heads of state and their mainstays squander the funds and suppress opposition, then there will be no progress at all. The majority of African heads of state are corrupt and I agree with Collier et al (2000) that one of the needs in Africa for economic development is appropriate democratic governance and high quality economic management. Democracy can only be initiated if a country believes in and agrees to act upon democratic ideals. Such ideals are not automatic but need to be taught and debated within the disciplines of the social sciences. Economic management needs an understanding of one's country's economic history, information and communications technology, policy analysts, statisticians, economists and other experts such as lawyers and environmentalists. This not only calls for the disciplines in the social sciences to play a role but an interdisciplinary approach, which requires a mutual infusion between the social sciences and other disciplines. Such possibilities would increase should Africa states strive towards general education and a multi- disciplinary approach to problem resolution.

One of the problems that have plunged Africa into deeper crisis than before is the AIDS epidemic and the growing prevalence of HIV infection among the youth and adult population. Sub-Saharan Africa alone accounts for more than 50 percent of adults and children living with HIV/AIDS. It has the highest percentage of women living with HIV, yet it is the only region in which the main mode of HIV transmission is heterosexual sexual intercourse. Of course the statistics are alarming, but the solutions are not as easy as simply using condoms, going for voluntary counselling and testing, and accessing antiretroviral drugs treatment. Medical technology is trying to develop drugs to cure, or vaccines to prevent HIV/AIDS. Progress in terms of antiretroviral drugs such as Zidovudine (AZT), Nevirapine, and Evafirenz and preventing mother to child transmission is pertinent. However, the social psychology and socio-cultural aspects of AIDS remain an important research task for the social sciences in Africa and elsewhere.

HIV/AIDS has social, political, economic and cultural dimensions that only disciplines in the social sciences can understand. In doing so they can guide interventions to curb the spread of the HIV virus. The first dimension that HIV/AIDS take is the historical and philosophical one. People often ask, 'where does this disease come from and why is it coming now?' While this question has a valid scientific interest, it also takes on social dimensions in that individuals struggle to make sense of the disease. Individuals often philosophise about the fact that it is chronic yet transmitted through sex which is supposed to be a natural activity. 'Why is AIDS incurable?' 'How are we supposed to procreate if we use condoms?' 'Is AIDS an indication of the imminence of the Judgement Day or Nemesis?' All these questions represent the conflation of fact and value. And it is through the skills of disciplines such as religious studies, sociology and history that interventions can be designed to try to inform the general population and hence help stop the spread of the virus.

HIV/AIDS also takes the personal dimension of people living with HIV/AIDS, and likewise of people taking care of people living with HIV/AIDS. The relationship between HIV and death is constant in the mind of an HIV positive person and those who take care of that person. For that matter, death is our ultimate fate. It turns into reality for someone living with a chronic disease such as AIDS. Technology and health sciences can only offer organic solutions. The mind, the spirit, the soul as elusive as they are, can best be dealt with in the disciplines of the social sciences such as social psychology, religious studies, medical sociology and cultural studies. It is the social sciences that need to continue to undertake research on the social relationships surrounding life and death. We need to know more about the cultural aspects of health, illness and death, on how people deal with grief, and cope with the fact that we are all mortal.

HIV/AIDS also has a macro-economic impact. The shortening life span of the economically active population and increasing absenteeism in the work place due to AIDS-related illnesses have a negative impact on economic productivity at the level of firms' output and gross national product. Jackson (2002:25) lists the following macro economic impact of HIV/AIDS:

-   Reduced national savings and investment, which are themselves critical for economic growth.
-   Increased spending on health at the expense of productive sector investment and spending.
-   Probable reduced spending on education, leading to slower skills accumulation and slower replacement of the labour force.

- Particularly heavy impacts on sectors dependent on professional, managerial, and skilled technical staff (who are costly and difficult to replace).
- Increased poverty and widening economic disparities as the poor are made even poorer.
- Changing markets in which the market for non-essentials will contract while those for items such as coffins will increase.
- The growth and increased reliance on the informal sector.
- Reduced economic efficiency (as institutional memory declines with the loss of experienced staff).
- Reduced capacity for governance (for the same reason).
- Increased national instability and social insecurity.

The long-term economic impact of HIV/AIDS needs to be resolved before it hits hard. Policy experts, economists, statisticians, labour unions, finance specialists, employer organisations, education specialists and researchers need to make informed proposals and interventions. Such proposals and interventions require expertise both in the social sciences and other disciplines. Synergy and multidisciplinary approaches cannot be more needed than in the case of HIV and AIDS.

While on the economic impact of HIV/AIDS on economies of developing countries, it is relevant to add that Third World debt owed to the International Monetary Fund (IMF) and the World Bank needs serious attention too. According to Jubilee Research (2003) the Heavily Indebted Poor Countries (HIPC) owe the IMF $7 billion, of which $2 billion will be cancelled by the IMF. HIPC also owe the World Bank $19.2 billion, of which $6 billion will be cancelled by the World Bank. Of course there have been debates about the origin and the impact of debt on Third World countries. There have also been calls for debt cancellation. For example, in the context

of South Africa, Madörin et al. writing for Jubilee 2000 South
Africa reckon that

> The people of southern Africa are still paying the cost of apart-
> heid. The physical and human costs of apartheid can still be
> seen in the neighbouring states where massive damage was
> caused by destabilisation, and in the former homelands and
> townships of South Africa itself. We believe it is immoral
> and unjustified that the people should pay twice for apart-
> heid... We thus urge those groups who supported our strug-
> gle against apartheid to now support our calls for the cancel-
> lation of apartheid-caused debt and for the payment of
> reparations by those who profited from our suffering (Madörin
> *et al* 1991: 1).

The burden of debt and the arguments in favour of debt
cancellation are not just about numbers and statistics. There
are moral, historical and developmental dimensions that need
to be constantly formulated, argued and revised. This implies
skills in critical thinking, knowledge of history and ethics,
economic, political and sociological analysis—almost the
entire range of skills of the disciplines within the social
sciences. The reconstruction of Africa and other developing
countries can neither be conceptualised nor executed without
the contribution of the social sciences. A good example of
good scholarship with regard to debt cancellation is a study
by Giyose (2003). He puts forward an argument against the
IMF's policy on debt cancellation. He draws a historical
comparison between the currently Heavily Indebted Poor
Countries conditions and their dealings with the IMF, and
the London Agreement on dealing with the debts of defeated
nations in World War II. He concludes that if the London
Agreement was to be applied to Third World debt, then it
could free countries from the debt burden. My point here is
not his argument but rather the method of analysis which is
atypical of angry 'scholarship' when it comes to issues such as

debt cancellation. He combines both history and critical analysis in soberly approaching a key developmental issue.

The debt crisis also comes at a critical time in which the negative effects of globalisation are more and more apparent in poor countries. Kunnie (2003) is critical of the discontents of globalisation. She writes:

> thanks to globalisation, the vulgarly obscene misadministra-
> tion of wealth and resources intensifies at a relentless pace.
> Today, the top 15 percent of the world, mostly the Western
> industrialized world, consumes 80 percent of the world re-
> sources. Twenty percent of the world's richest countries re-
> ceive 1.4 percent of the world's income, (Kunnie 2003:5).

She goes on to demonstrate the global inequalities in terms of income inequality and unequal benefits in trade. She then concludes that developing countries need to respond to such exploitation by activism and intellectual struggles through research and good scholarship. She also lashes out at social science scholarship that is characterised by emotivism and defensive undertones. While it is not clear if she is not essentialising Africa, she does advocate an interdisciplinary approach in the struggle against globalisation.

In response to the challenges posed by globalisation, the establishment of the African Union and the New Economic Partnership for Development (NEPAD) currently exempli- fies the reconstruction of Africa for Africa's development. Of course not everyone is happy about the two institutions. Some see the AU as the old OAU with a new name, while others see hope in the African Renaissance. Some view NEPAD as a new development for Africa to strengthen economic ties with the West, others see it as global neo-liberalism to further the exploitation of developing countries by developed ones. Either way such issues require informed debates with critical thinking. They require critical perspectives on how we see the world and how we want it to be. They require new ways of analysis in disciplines such as literature, media studies, sociology, history, art, economics, and philosophy.

Conclusion

I have argued that Africa needs the social sciences more than ever before. The social sciences have been used to counteract colonial discourse about Africa. However, I have disagreed with the essentialism that has characterised social science scholarship in Africa. I then argued for an approach in the social sciences that is both critical and multidisciplinary so that diversity could be appreciated and form part of scholarship in Africa.

Bibliography

Bates, R., Mudimbe, V., and O'Barr, J., 1993, *Africa and the Disciplines*, Chicago: University of Chicago Press.

Bell, R., 2002, *Understanding African Philosophy: A Cross-Cultural Approach to Classical and Contemporary Issues*, London: Routledge.

Collier, P., Elbadawi, I., Sambanis, N., 2000, *The Economics of Crime and Violence*, Washington DC, World Bank, http://www.eldis.org/static/DOC7755.htm, accessed 25 October 2003).

Department of Education, 1997, *Education White Paper 3: A Programme for the Transformation of Higher Education*, Pretoria: Department of Education.

Diop, C.A., 1996, *Towards the African Renaissance: Essays in African Culture & Development: 1946-1960*, London: Karnak House.

Dowling, K.W., 1998, 'Utilitarianism, the Social Sciences and the University Curriculum', *Bulletin: News for the Human Sciences*, Vol. 5, 1(6-8).

Eagleson, I., 2002, 'The Global History of African Music: The Kenyan Song "Malaika"', in T. Falola, (ed.) *Africanising Knowledge: African Studies Across the Disciplines*, London: Transaction Press.

Falola, T., 2002, *Africanising Knowledge: African Studies Across the Disciplines*, London: Transaction Publishers.

Garland, D., 1995, *The Eye of the Beholder: Deformity and Disability in Graeco-Roman World*, London: Duckworth.

Giyose, M., 2003, 'Forgive Us This Day Our Odious Debt', New Agenda: *South African Journal of Social and Economic Policy*, Issue 11, p.57.

Jackson, H., 2002, 'The AIDS Epidemic', in *AIDS Africa: Continent in Crisis*, Harare: SafAIDS.

Jubilee Research, 2003, 'Can the World Bank and the IMF Cancel 100% of Poor Country Debt?', www.jubileeresearch.org, accessed 20 October 2003.

July, R.W., 1987, *An African Voice: The Role of the Social Sciences in African Independence*, Durham: Duke University Press.

Kunnie, J., 2003, 'Globalisation: A Recolonization of Africa', paper presented at the Graduate School for Social sciences with the Centre for African Studies, University of Cape Town, 13 August.

Lange, L., 1998, 'History and Memory', *Bulletin: News for the Human Sciences*, Vol. 5, 1(6-8).

Madörin, M., Wellmer, G., and Egil, M., 1999, *Apartheid-Caused Debt: The Role of German and Swiss Finance*, Pretoria: Jubilee 2000 South Africa.

Mamdani, M., 1996, 'Introduction: Thinking through Africa's Impasse', in Citizen and Subject, New Jersey: Princeton University Press.

Mamdani, M., 1998, 'Is African Studies to be Turned into a New Home for Bantu Education at UCT?', Seminar Debates Controversial Africa Course, unpublished paper.

Marks, S., 2000, 'The Role of the Social Sciences in Higher Education in South Africa', seminar paper presented at the Graduate School for Social Sciences with Centre for African Studies, University of Cape Town.

Mazrui, A.A., 1986, 'Cultural Forces in African Politics', in I.J. Mowoe and R. Bjornson, eds., *Africa and the West*, New York: Greenwood Press.

Masolo, D.A., 2002, 'Logocentrism and Emotivism', in *African Philosophy in Search of Identity*, Edinburgh: Edinburgh University Press.

Moore, S., 1993, 'Changing Perspectives on a Changing Africa', in R. Bates, V. Modime, and J. O'Barr, eds., *Africa and the Disciplines*, Chicago: University of Chicago Press.

Mzamane, M.V., 1998, 'Cultural Studies and Nation Building', *Bulletin: News for the Human Sciences*, Vol. 5, 1(6-8).

Nel, J.E., and van der Westhuizen, P.C., 1998, 'Programme-based Education within the Social Sciences: Ostranenie Revisited?', *Bulletin: News for the Human Sciences*, Vol. 5, 1(6-8).

Nketia, J.H.K., 1986, 'Perspectives on African Musicology', in I. J. Mowoe, and R. Bjornson, eds., *Africa and the West*, New York: Greenwood Press.

Nketia, J.H.K., 1994, 'Reorganising African Social Sciences in Africa', paper presented at the Rockefeller Foundation meeting on the State of Social Sciences in Africa, Nairobi, Kenya, November 29-December 1.

Oliver, M., 1990, *Politics of Disablement*, Basingstoke, Macmillan Education.

Oliver, M., 1996, *Understanding Disability—From Theory to Practice*, Basingstoke: Macmillan.

Rostow, W., 1960, 'The Five Stages of Economic Growth - A Summary', in Roberts, B., Cushing, R. and Wood, C., eds., *The Sociology of Development*, Volume 1, Aldershot: Edward Elgar Publishing.

Silwimba, F., 'Possibilities of Independent Living of Persons with Disabilities in Africa', http://www.independentliving.org/toolsforpower/tools5.html, accessed October 20, 2003.

Task Force on Education and Society, 2000, *Higher Education in Developing Countries*, Washington D.C.: World Bank.

Thomson, G., ed., 1996, *Freakery: Cultural Aspects of the Extraordinary Body*, New York: New York University Press.

The Social Sciences and Africa's Development: Between Construction and Deconstruction

Claude Abé

The Social Sciences and the Development of Human Societies

This paper focuses on the need for the social sciences in Africa. It examines the role of disciplines that fall under the umbrella of the social sciences, from the standpoint of their practice on the continent. We will, specifically, assess the importance of the social sciences by determining the use and effectiveness of their contribution in meeting the contemporary challenges facing this part of the global village.[1]

Indeed, the question of the relationship between the social sciences and social action has been investigated since time immemorial; the case of sociology alone sufficiently illustrates this point (Simon 1999:46). As early as 1819, A. Comte, who coined the term 'sociology', wrote to one of his friends:

> Let us keep in touch with human beings so as to contribute to the improvement of their lot. My work is, and will be, two-fold: scientific and political. I would give very little credit to scientific work if I were not continually thinking of its utility (Cited by P.-J. Simon 1999:47).

The same commitment to contribute to the development of
society underpins the objective which E. Durkheim, the father
of French sociology, ascribes to his work. This is the
commitment he expresses when he asserts:

> Thus, we propose, above all, to study reality; this does not
> mean that we are abandoning the idea of improving on it;
> our research would not be worth an hour's trouble if its util-
> ity were merely speculative. If we take pains to draw the line
> between theoretical and practical problems, it is not with a
> view to neglecting the latter; on the contrary, it is to put our-
> selves in a position to solve them (1986: xxxviii-ix).

The relationship between sociology and social development
was also one of the major concerns of the founders of the
discipline in Germany. One of the works of Max Weber, the
father of German sociology, is a study on 'the vocation of
science in all human life' (1959:71). In *Science as a
Vocation*(1959), Weber establishes the function of sociology
in promoting socio-economic development by defining the
respective roles of the social science researcher and the
politician: the former contributes to social progress by means
of the knowledge he produces while the latter is in charge of
applying it through social reform.

To avoid reducing the social sciences solely to sociology
(Bourdieu and Wacquant 1992) by viewing it as a field of
illustration, we can say that previous developments are proof
that the central argument in this paper, i.e. the relationship
between the social sciences and social progress, is an age-old
preoccupation. In this light, it is, therefore, not the originality
of the subject under study that justifies this study. It is justified
by two factors: the renewed interest in the subject and the
topical nature of scientific preoccupations in Africanist
research.

On the whole, there has been renewed interest in the
relationship between the social sciences and social

development over the past two decades. There is abundant literature showing the various uses of knowledge generated by the social sciences with a view to boosting the sagging world economy (Chanlat 1998; de Coster 1999; *L'Homme et la Société* 1999; Wieviorka 1998; Crozier 2000). We observe the 'routinisation' (Giddens 1987) of this scientific pre-occupation. Such self-evident 'routinisation' is an indication that the choice of the theme of this study was neither by chance nor out of imagination. Assessing the importance of the social sciences in promoting socio-economic and political progress is justified by the need to successfully link this issue to the burning issues in the social sciences. The current logic of Africanist studies is also partly related to this choice and the urgent need for the Council for the Development of Social Science Research in Africa (CODESRIA) to take stock of the ground covered, as it celebrates thirty years of research and knowledge production in the social sciences.

The time has come to assess the practice of the social sciences in Africa, almost half a century after it first begun. There is abundant literature on the subject (read Copans 1990; Copans 2000; and the journal, *L'homme et la société*, 1986). Although such a fashionable practice can be contested to justify our choice, we, nevertheless, consider it sufficient. In this study, we have used it as a basis for reflection on the situation in Africa, in light of the status of the social sciences on the continent. This is an innovative question that has hitherto been little explored, in particular, from the point of view of the relationship between the social sciences and development in African societies (Ela 1998).

Nevertheless, the socio-economic and political situation in Africa has for long been studied by researchers. Such realities are part and parcel of the people who are the focus of social science researchers on the continent. From disease (Sindzingre 1983; Brunet-Jailly and Rougemont 1989; Jaffré and De Sardan

1999) to politics—(for an inventory of works in this area in
Africa, see Bakary 1992)—and, of course, the economy (see
Amin 1985, 1989; Mahieu 1990; Requier-Desjardins 1989) or
history (Coquery-Vidrovitch 1972, 1988, 1985, 1999; Bénot
1995; Balandier 1981), Africa has been studied for at least
half a century. This multidisciplinary scientific investment is
aimed at studying phenomena related to such age-old fields
of action, that is, to know them with a view to explaining and
understanding them. There is no shortage of research work
designed to explain the situation in Africa. There are, by and
large, three types of explanations: it is common practice to
blame local traditions and cultures (Kabou 1991; Etounga-
Manguèllè 1993), trade imbalances between the Africa and
Western countries (Amin 1985 and 1989; Ela 1990 and 1998)
or, even more conveniently, practices of African governments
(Médard 1983 and 1986; Bayart 1989; Bayart *et al* 1997;
Mbembe 1999 and 2000). All such avenues for explaining the
real situation lead to the same conclusion: the breakdown of
Africa (Giri 1985, also see Dumont 1962).

However, the Burkinabe historian, Joseph Ki-Zerbo, who
opens up another hitherto unexplored avenue for reflection,
argues and points out that if there is a breakdown, it should
not be attributed to the continent but rather to the practice
of the social sciences in Africa. He, specifically, writes that
'[Africa] is currently paralyzed by concepts and theories that
function as rigid and unilateral models of analysis and action
aimed at 'understanding' our continent as part of a system or
dominant systems' (1992: 2). Beyond Ki-Zerbo's critical view
of the practice of the social sciences in Africa is a strong
assertion of their role as the driving force of the continent's
development. According to Ki-Zerbo's perspective, there is a
correlation between the development of research and that of
the continent as a whole; as a result of such 'functional

correlation' (Elias 1990:84), the mediocrity of local research appears to be a reflection of Africa's paralysis.

Without doubting the relevance of the above analysis, I would like to comment on Ki-Zerbo's point of view, in light of what we have learnt from the history of the correlation between research and development elsewhere, especially in the developed countries. The case of France is an example. In 1978, a report of the OECD (Organisation for Economic Co-operation and Development) found that there was a gap between France's scientific performance and its economic development; almost ten years later, another study by the same organization reached the same conclusion (OECD 1986). In 1998, the same findings were echoed in the Guillaume Report on the paradox between scientific production and economic performance (Guillaume 1998). This shows that the link between development and scientific research is not automatic. Be that as it may, does the situation in the continent go hand-in-hand with that of social science research in Africa? In other words, does the status of knowledge and that of the practice of the social sciences in Africa account for the continent's underdevelopment? Can Africa's development be mechanically linked to the development of the social sciences? Or, to what extent can we say that the transformation of Africa's socio-historic situation in the interest of Africans depends on the fortunes of the social sciences on the continent? Should the funding of social science research be viewed as an investment in the improvement of the living conditions of African people?

To answer the above questions, we postulate that the balance between the development of the social sciences in Africa and the transformation/improvement of the socio-economic and political situation is a complex equation that cannot be solved mechanically. Although progress in local research is the most important factor in the promotion of socio-economic development, it is primarily part of a system of interdependent and dependent components of diverse parameters that contribute towards creating/triggering development.

To discuss the above hypothesis, we have sub-divided this reflection into two major parts. The first part shows how the social sciences are an indispensable development tool both in Africa and elsewhere. The main idea here is that Africa's breakdown is the consequence of that of the social sciences on the continent. It is now established that work in the social sciences, in particular, the intelligibility and 'knowledge of the laws that govern society and history... enable us to foresee and, perhaps, to take preventive action... Indeed, insufficient knowledge of such laws coupled with erudite ignorance, so to speak, is fertile ground for the birth and development of political and social utopias whose implementation is a nightmare' (Grignon 2002:133). The second part of the study shows the non-mechanistic nature of the relationship between the social sciences and development in the African context. The point made by Lahire in respect of sociology, that 'its extra-scientific utility...partly depends on its social recognition as legitimate scientific discourse', applies to all the disciplines that come under the umbrella of the social sciences (2002:44). Such recognition is in itself related to the degree of empirical accuracy in knowledge production, that is, the relevance of the scientific works in this area (Lahire 2002:44).

Our research, though mainly documentary, derives some of its data from spontaneous observation of daily experiences in African situations. This kind of observation, which M. Grawitz describes as unsystematic, consists in accumulating 'involuntarily or, at least, in a more or less marginal manner, observations that can lead to a research orientation or idea' (2001:395). It is a specific approach involving the collection of 'meaningful facts in the area of observation' (Grawitz 2001:395), without a pre-conceived tool.

Part I

Breakdown in Social Development or Crisis of Knowledge Society for the Development of African

This part sets out to highlight, by hindsight, the need for the social sciences in the development of Africa. It is a comparative study of the socio-economic and political situation in African countries, on the one hand, and the status of research in this field from 1960 to 1992, on the other. The choice of this period is not by chance or imagination; it is premised on the need to identify relevant reference points: 1960 is the year when most African countries gained independence with its cohort of promises of economic and political development. Earmarking that year as a reference point further highlights the need to take stock of the ground covered up to 1992, that is, the time when the West imposed Structural Adjustment Programmes and all sorts of conditions on African countries (Mappa 1995).

More precisely, this part is a cross-analysis of experiments in development and the evolution of the social sciences in Africa. The question here is whether underdevelopment in the practice of and recourse to the social sciences could ultimately account for the difficulties encountered in the social production of development on the continent. If the answer is yes, we would rely on the 'circular vision of the construction of the society' (Corcuff 1995:49), which is a hallmark of the 'reflexive sociology' of Giddens (1987:15), to prove that the situation in Africa is the consequence of that of the social sciences since the latter influences development, including that of the continent.

The development of the social sciences in Africa is viewed here from two angles, in regard to its contribution in initiating and guiding actions aimed at improving living conditions on the continent: like the structuralist approach, it is both 'constraining and enabling' (Giddens 1987:226), an obstacle and a possibility. In this paper, the development of the social sciences is viewed at the outset as a structuring pre-requisite for the socio-economic and political development of the continent before the start of this experiment, and the status of the latter appears as a finished product. This is the analytical perspective offered when we tap into the dual nature of the structuralist approach as a possible explanation of reality through Giddens' theory of structuration: according to this theory, 'the structural properties of social systems are both conditions and results of activities carried out by agents who are part of such systems' [unofficial translation] (Giddens 1987:15). What is envisaged here is, therefore, not a study of history in light of Giddens' sociology.

A Beleaguered African Continent

Socio-Political Situation

The greatest socio-political challenge facing most African countries when they gained independence in the 1960s was national construction, that is, developing a viable political system and community. At the outset, a strategy was adopted to attain that goal. The strategy chosen in most cases was a centralized State with a strong executive geared towards the achievement of the goal of national unity. While 'the new sub-Saharan African States which gained independence in the 1960s forged their emancipation in the parliamentary mould' (Conac 1993:12), the second half of the 1960s was marked by the devalorisation of such innate consti-tutionalism (Conac 1993:12) and the abandonment of inherent political pluralism.

That was the era when one-party regimes were adopted wholesale, with the attendant ills such as restrictions of civic freedoms. In this regard, two major techniques were experimented: custom and law. Some countries like Cameroon and Côte d'Ivoire did not have to change their constitution: here, the technique consisted in making the fundamental (law, ineffective in its most essential provisions through the emergence of a de facto single party' (Conac 1993:13). Others, like Zaire (now the Democratic Republic of Congo), Guinea-Conakry or Angola, preferred to adopt a new constitution to legitimate presidential absolutism.

Several reasons were advanced to justify the one-party option (Conac 1993:12-13). In brief, they can be grouped under three categories. The first is the Marxist position premised on the incompatibility of multiparty politics with a revolutionary conception of power. That is the position held by Guinea-Conakry's Sékou Touré and Sassou Nguesso of Congo-Brazzaville. The second is the argument of the constraints of national unity: most of the former French colonies see an instrumental value in adopting the single party. Here, the advent of the one-party regime was a response to a constraint—that of nation-building—rather than to a whim. The third set of reasons often advanced is that which justified the adoption of the single party as a development imperative; from that standpoint, the country needed to rally its elites around certain objectives.

Yet, thirty years later, at the dawn of the 1990s, there was neither nation nor development—nothing had been built. The nation-state project resulted in the privatization of power in a number of cases (see Médard 1983; Kamto 1987; Bayart 1985; Lootvoet 1996). Such privatization of power in turn ushered in control of public affairs paving the way for corruption and racketeering (Médard 1998; Mbembe 1999). The main observation that can be made on that period is that it was a time of genuine self-denial, in particular, denial of the differences between the various social groups that were

muzzled in the name of national unity (see Fogui 1990).
However, stifling the differences did not result in their self-
effacement or abandonment in favour of a satellite identity,
an umbrella identity encompassing even groups of a lesser
identity. As Bourgi and Casteran rightly point out, 'ethnic
rivalries are always in the background of the political debate'
(1991:22; also read Scarrit and Mozzafar 1999; Diaw 1994).
The extreme case of the 1994 Rwandan genocide (Prunier
1995) or the distressing demolition of Somalia (Leymarie
1994) testify to the relevance of this remark.

It was a difficult period because of the law of silence
imposed on all citizens, irrespective of leaning. That law
translated into violations of freedoms (Mbembe 1985). One
of the most visible faces of the policy of non-recognition of
freedoms is imprisonment without trial. All that led to ruthless
policing and negation of civil society (Bourgi and Casteran
1991:17; Conac 1993; Bayart 1992). In view of Africa's
economic situation at the dawn of the 1990s, in particular,
the poor living conditions in most social groups, one would
agree with Bourgi and Casteran that 'the one-party system
has failed to achieve the purpose for which it was instituted'
(1991:23): development.

Economic situation

After thirty years of experimenting in development and self-
government, the economic situation is bleak; the economy
has collapsed and needs to be overhauled. At the beginning
of the 1990s, all efforts were geared towards accommodating
the challenges inherited from the economic situation of the
1980s; as a result of such a heritage, African economies could
only struggle to stay afloat, since they could not possibly hope
for anything better, in view of the constraints imposed by the
said challenges.

One of the most rampant challenges is the endemic poverty affecting 10 percent of the world's population living in Africa. Apart from having the highest levels of poverty, Africa also has the highest percentage of the world's poor, that is, people living below the poverty line, in a state of psychological, socio-political impoverishment (Friedmann and Sandercock 1995:15) and total deprivation. To visualize the situation, it suffices to recall that 'Africa has 33 of the 48 Least Developed Countries (LDC) and 36 out of the 45 countries with a low Human Development Index (HDI) (Hugon 2000:18). Food insecurity is one of the most visible facets to such deprivation and destitution. Indeed, under-nourishment is rampant in Africa. It is estimated that the number of the under-nourished increased from 101 million in 1969–1971 to 168 million in 1988–90, representing about a third of the African population (Northoff 1993:73). The number of the under-nourished living in Africa is estimated at 180 million (Hugon 2000:18). The problem is rooted in the drop in per capita food production; in the 1980s, it dropped by 2 percent (Northoff 1993:73). In 1982, food production fell to an all-time low and large numbers perished as a result of severe famine on the continent (Onitri 1990:49). After twenty years of experimenting, the food situation in Africa is so precarious and alarming that States have resorted to emergency food aid; the case of Ethiopia is forever etched on people's minds. The famine was the result of severe drought and possibly an indirect consequence of the political conflicts that rocked African countries in the late 1980s (Anon 2000:10).

Scarcity or deprivation is also a characteristic of the job market. The early 1980s were marked by a deep-seated crisis in employment structures. The difficulties encountered by the public and private sectors led to significant job losses. In Cameroon, for instance, during the period from 1987 to 1991, 58,689 workers lost their jobs, with 37,778 of them (i.e. 64.4

percent) being due to layoffs. The 12 biggest state corporations in the country accounted for 15 percent of the layoffs (Kobou 1999:133). The situation was similar in the Democratic Republic of Congo. There, too, the job market has, since the mid-1970s, been in a crisis affecting both the public and private sectors (Biaya 2000:32). In Senegal, the employment situation has been aggravated by increasing job losses and significant cuts in employment by the State, which is the main employer (Fall 1997). The all-pervading crisis in the job market has affected all African countries, including even those considered to be the continent's economic giants. Nigeria, hit by a severe form of unemployment, is a good case in point (Nnoli 1993). Such examples are indicators of the employment situation in African countries in the late 1980s.

The worsening socio-economic situation is compounded by Africa's increasing dependence. The situation can easily be explained by analysis of Africa's economic development: African countries are still revenue-based (Hugon 1999) and outward-looking economies (Bayart 1999), as industrialization remains rudimentary, in contrast with the exponential increase in its foreign debt. In addition to such under-development, which warranted the futile Structural Adjustment Programmes (Hugon 1993), Africa also has to cope with its 20 million children affected by AIDS and, in particular, its disconnection from international trade, which is part and parcel of globalisation (Abé 2001). Such disconnection is evident in its volume of trade with the rest of the world, in particular, the West. With Africa's share of world trade representing only 2 percent, while the percentage of direct investments is almost nil (1 percent)—(for detailed figures, see Hugon 2000:18)— it is obvious that Africa has fallen by the wayside in the current global economy. This observation ties in with that of Bourgi and Casteran: 'Not needed by the global economy, abandoned by the super powers, neglected on account of outdated ideological rivalries, Africa is now all by itself' (1991:24).

One of the causes of such marginalization is the continent's indebtedness. The image bandied about everywhere is that of a continent on drips, that is to say, living solely on handouts from donors and the Bretton Woods Institutions. A few examples would suffice to give an idea of the prevailing situation at the dawn of the 1990s. 'In 1992, Mali's foreign debt stood at CFA800 billion (FF16 billion)' (*Le Monde* 1992:100), that is, about four times its budget for that year. The situation in Cameroon was hardly different from that of Mali; in 1992, Cameroon's foreign debt was CFA1,500 billion (*Le Monde* 1992:102), an indebtedness which prompted financial institutions to ignore the country. Gabon, too, because of its huge foreign debt, had considerable difficulty honouring its commitments towards its creditors, to whom it owed CFA 809 billion in 1992, 'with debt service alone representing CFA 384.5 billion—almost the equivalent of its budget' (*Le Monde* 1992:103).

In view of the financial difficulties faced by African countries, international financial institutions and donors are increasingly losing faith in Africa. As a result of such loss of confidence, the continent is being left to its own devices. African countries, unable to rely on themselves, also cannot qualify for 'debt relief' (Ekoué Amaïzo 2001:28). Like Cameroon, a number of African countries are excluded from foreign aid. In the Central African Republic, civil servants went without salaries for months before being laid off. Africa has also lost access to non-debt-generating resources as a result of the crisis of confidence in the international money market. People now refer to Africa as a strangled continent (Dumont 1982).

The only sector that still sustains the illusion of the proverbial light at the end of the tunnel—because it seems to be growing and offering opportunities to the resourceful (Biaya 2000:34)—is the popular urban economy, generally referred to as the informal or unstructured sector. This sector, which 'employs the overwhelming majority of people' (Diouf 1998: 19) is a smokescreen to the deepening economic crisis (Abé 2001:326-27; Diouf 1998:19).

In brief, it is obvious that the development promised and legitimately awaited has not been delivered. The results are disappointing; as a result of poverty, the debt burden, the collapse in world prices of raw materials, growing unemployment, marginal contribution from foreign aid (Onitri 1990:49), etc., African economies are in a shambles at a time of scarce resources, wide-ranging difficulties and marginalization. To borrow Egyptian economist Samir Amin's favourite expression, 'Africa's development has broken down' (1989). The economic situation is closely related to the socio-political situation analyzed above. This is a clear indication that the first thirty years of independence have only left Africa saddled with a wide range of problems.

This said, instead of simply pointing an accusing finger at the system of management of public affairs—as practically everyone has done so far—can it be said that the situation of research and knowledge production in the social sciences is the cause of the difficulties? In other words, is Africa's performance a reflection of the performance of the social sciences in terms of explaining reality? We will now attempt to answer that question.

The Social Sciences in Africa: Lessons from the Past

Situational Analysis

This section explains the African situation we have just described in terms of that of the social sciences on the continent. There are two or three areas of observation: one is the status of this discipline in Africa, compared to the situation in the developed countries with regard to staffing, and the other is the responsibility of scholars specializing in this domain of knowledge production, in particular, the political democratization process and promotion of development.

Although the social sciences attract scant attention, compared to disciplines such as mathematics and physics, for instance (Ela 1994:8; Diouf 1982:164), there is no shortage of social science educational and research infrastructure on the continent (Mbonigaba Mugaruka *et al.*, 1982). Apart from specialized research centres such as Institut français d'Afrique noire (IFAN) [French Institute of Black African Studies] in Dakar or Institut des sciences humaines (ISH) [Institute of Social Sciences] in Yaounde, to name but a few, the social sciences are taught in university faculties and institutions of higher learning such as the Ecole normale [Higher Teacher Training College] or the School of Administration. Nevertheless, there is an acute shortage of human resources.

Generally, the staff employed in research and teaching of the social sciences in Africa during the first thirty years of independence was insufficient. The work of Joseph Ki-Zerbo gives us an idea of the situation:

> The number of African scientists and engineers working in Research and Development represents only 0.4% of the world total, compared to 11.2% for all the developing countries in 1980. The per capita index of scientists and engineers working in Research and Development in Africa (except for the Arab countries) was estimated at 49 in 1980, compared to 127 for all the developing countries and 2,986 for the developed countries. Africa's share of scientific works stands at 0.3, compared to 0.96 for Latin America and 94% for countries of the North. Such percentages are practically stagnant in the case of Africa (1992:8).

In the social sciences, the shortage of staff is even more glaring. The situation can be illustrated by three cases. In Benin, there are very few specialists in this discipline (Aguessy 1982:48). The situation is the same in Cameroon (Ndoumbé Manga and Endaman 1982:60) and in Senegal (Diouf 1982:164). We could, on the basis of such findings, postulate that the number of social scientists directly impacts the socio-economic development of a country. The development gap between developing countries and developed countries can be explained in terms of the number of social scientists working in the field.

The history of development in developed countries offers many lessons on the importance of human resources in the development process. As Jackson rightly observes, 'Today, science and technology are the key to capital development. To develop, countries need highly qualified manpower' (2000:54). In the case of Africa, 'one of the keys to posing the problems correctly...and, therefore, to answering them validly is the concept of local development. In this regard, the word "development"—which is so ambiguous—should never be used without the qualifier "endogenous", which adds a positive ingredient to it' (Ki-Zerbo 1992:1). To make development endogenous, that is to say, linked to the context in which it is conducted, bearing in mind socio-cultural specificities, we must be able to identify the structural components of the local tradition, history and culture (Drucker 1990:135-136). Such work can only be done by social scientists. That is why in Africa, when we talk of highly qualified staff for the implementation of development projects, we mean social scientists.

The lesson we can, therefore, learn from the quantitative data provided by Ki-Zerbo is that there is a cause-effect relationship, a strong correlation/link between knowledge production and the size of the social science workforce in Research and Development, on the one hand, and the economic performance of a country or continent, on the other.

Indeed, the percentages show that the greater the human resources in this particular branch of research, the greater the presence of researchers in the field of knowledge production and the stronger the economy. In light of the foregoing, we can say that the difficulties encountered by Africa are the consequence of insufficient Research and Development staff; such a shortage of staff also explains Africa's inadequate contribution to knowledge production in the social sciences. We will return later to the causes of such a situation by examining government policies relating to the promotion of the social sciences in Africa.

Again, to show that the African situation is, to a large extent, a function of the status of the social sciences on the continent, we will focus on the responsibility of specialists in this field of knowledge production. As we stressed above, African countries gained independence in a context of political pluralism but the latter soon gave way to one-party regimes obsessed with policing civil society, often at the cost of 'physically eliminating or exiling a large proportion of their population' (Lootvoet 1996:85; Le Pensec 1988:94-6). Unfortunately, African intellectuals were not spared by the technology for manufacturing silence through all sorts of intimidation, including even imprisonment or, which is more serious, political assassination (Kom 1993:61-8).

If we stopped at the above observation, we would conclude that as a result of the reining in of university communities by African central governments (Adarelegbé 1991:69-91), the modest and timid contribution of social scientists to the political development of the continent is understandable, especially taking into account the size of the workforce in that area. However, such an analysis could prove ludicrous since it is far removed from the reality. First, that proposition gives the impression that all African intellectuals are in the government opposition. Yet, all African intellectuals are not outside the corridors of power. Further, as Mamdani observes, whatever may be the side on which they are, social scientists have hardly distanced themselves from the fundamental positions of the elite in power (1994:278). For instance, the analysis of their work shows that, regardless of their relationship with government, they have an aversion for democracy and political pluralism and agree with the ruling class that development must come from the top rather than from the bottom, as required in a participatory process (Mamdani 1994:278-82). This again shows the extent of the responsibility the social scientist had to assume in the African situation at the dawn of the 1990s. To illustrate this argument, let us consider only the hijacking and manipulation of social scientists working in Research and Development on the continent.

Indeed, notwithstanding the shortage of staff which makes it impossible to conduct any significant research and development, a number of social scientists 'are in government: in some cases they form the hardcore of the State apparatus but do not deem it necessary to discharge, by themselves, their duty to produce knowledge or to delegate such a duty which is, after all, the first definition of the social position' (Copans 1990:230). Ochwada cites the case of Kenya with a view to explaining the functioning of such 'Government intellectuals' (Ochwada 1997:42-3); he points out that in Kenya, such intellectuals do not stop at the legitimization of government corruption and patronage; 'they even sang the praises of the leaders when the latter erred' (1997:42). Those are the Apparatchiks, the sycophants of authoritarian regimes in power; those are the people helping to keep them in power and to perpetuate dictatorship as a legitimate form of government in Africa. This means that their know-how, at least, has been used to preserve the status quo instead of helping to reform the rules of governance and, thereby, institute democratic governance.

Such an attitude on the part of some social scientists does not at all reflect a failure on the part of the social sciences, per se. It can be understood through the following analogy with the natural sciences. The use of the atom bomb in Hiroshima and Nagasaki to destroy human life did not herald the failure of the natural sciences but their betrayal by the users of the said sciences. The same analogy can be drawn in respect of social scientists who become Apparatchiks. In this sense, their conduct brings to the fore instead the consequences of a particular use of that field of knowledge by career-oriented scholars; if we subscribe to the role which Durkheim and Comte have assigned to producers of knowledge in the social sciences, which is, to contribute, through such activity, in improving the living conditions of the people they study, the said attitude can be understood as an illustration of the underdevelopment of the social sciences in Africa. It is, therefore, pure surrender and cowardly resignation (Caillé 1993) from their duties, for social scientists to adhere, without any sense of detachment, the State apparatus which is undoubtedly responsible for the African crisis. This is further evidence that the situation of the social sciences reflects that of the continent. Thus, the problems besetting the continent can be viewed as a consequence of the betrayal of the social sciences (Benda 1965) by the main players in that discipline. Such betrayal runs counter to the purpose of social science research since it sustains and maintains a system of governance that is unfavourable to the development of African countries.

In light of the foregoing, we see the interrelation between the status of the social sciences and economic and socio-political performances on the African continent, in particular, in sub-Saharan Africa: the under-development of the social sciences mirrors the wide-ranging difficulties described above—the latter being a consequence of the former. In so far as the development of the social sciences heralds and influences the development of the African continent, as we have just seen, it is not an exaggeration to join Ki-Zerbo in arguing that to develop the social sciences in Africa is to develop the continent. This argument is also substantiated by the parallelism between the practice of the social sciences in Africa and the situation of the continent.

The Unproductiveness of the Social Sciences in Africa

We have just shown that the underdevelopment of the social sciences in Africa resulted from the environment in which they were practised. Nevertheless, our analysis would be incomplete, superficial and hence biased, if it went no further and failed to examine practitioners inherent in their practice within that environment. Indeed, a thorough and objective examination of how the social sciences were practised on the continent in the first thirty years of independence can bring to light cogent elements that argue that the social sciences were themselves also responsible for their own 'political atony' (Caillie 1993:16). The hypothesis being examined here posits that the under-developed practice of the social sciences in Africa negatively affected the economic and political take-off of countries on the continent. Much more narrowly, it entails assessing the consequences that a certain way of conducting the social sciences had on attempts to develop Africa. To that end, we have retained only three salient aspects of this practice: the failure to adjust view points, the love of post-mortems and the overwhelming State control apparent in the analysis of works.

A curious practice of the social sciences prevailed in Africa during the first thirty years of independence. It consisted of dispensing with 'an analysis of processes inherent in each concept' (Bidima 2000:92). As an illustration, the concept of development was often used in an uncontrolled manner in works. When Kabou argues that Africans refuse development (1991) or when Etounga Manguelle takes up the same argument, believing that Africa needs a cultural adjustment (1993), they are surely talking about modernization. Such confusion between modernization and development is further evident in the title of an article by Manguelle which sets out to demonstrate his argument using the example of Cameroon (1995). He argues that Cameroon's under-development is one of the 'resultants of the late modernization of our social systems' (1995:74). Yet, as Copans very aptly demonstrates, modernization is different from development and vice versa (1990:226-35). While one—modernization—is an 'imposed and extraneous acquisition of disembodied and inchoate features' (1990:227), the other—development—constitutes a 'pristine and native product of modernity' (1990:229).

The error made by studies hugging closely the views propounded by Kabou and Etounga Manguelle was their adoption of concepts without the wholesome benefit of hindsight. And 'in this administration of concepts, reflection— a painful process of opening thought to itself and to things alien to itself—is no longer subjected to the hesitation, doubt and probing that attended its presuppositions' (Bidima 2000:90). Such practice of the social sciences also dispensed with genuine field research and instead indulged in loud-sounding declarations which were more of monstrations than demonstrations (see Medard's critique of the school of popular modes of political action, 1994; also Sindjoun 2002:2-3). The end-result of this way of conducting research is that it culminates in 'a desocialized view of social life' (Wieviorka 2000:11) as was seen earlier on with Kabou and Etounga Manguelle. This is also what Sindjoun notices when he blames studies, which analyze African political life solely by using '(exotic) categories of derision and simulacrum', for their failure to attune their viewpoint to the reality to be observed in the field of social experience (2002:3).

Now, field experience is what precisely makes reflection on a concept possible, especially by subjecting day-to-day realities to the test. This is what emerges from an analysis of works such as that of the French anthropologist Copans who, by comparing the concept of development with reality, came to the conclusion that 'so-called 'development' policies ... instead of accelerating maturation, cynically cause an internal festering' (Copans 1990:231). This means that the way social sciences were practised in Africa in the past led to significant deprivation. Since the practice of the social sciences lacked critical and insightful analysis, active knowledge-seeking agents were deprived of the endogenous anthropological infrastructure—sort of building blocks serving as basic structural elements in the formulation of relevant development actions. It is on this score that this practice becomes a factor explaining the failures recorded in the first thirty years of attempts to develop Africa. The underdevelopment of African societies thus stands as ample publicity of the underdeveloped practice of social sciences in Africa. The correlation between these and the development of the continent thus becomes apparent.

Another argument in support of this view is a logic inherent in the practice of the social sciences. This logic, requiring that the researcher distance himself temporally (Elias 1997:355-83; Sindjoun 1999:1-3), led to a research tradition in Africa which showed a marked preference for retrospective studies in the development domain. In most cases, the social sciences only stepped in once the action was over, as the intention and objective here was to assess and explain the failures recorded during the implementation of a development project or programme (Boiral 1985:47). It contributed in isolating them from the field of action, and crystallized them as a field of knowledge which had become unproductive because totally out of touch with the actual concerns of the societies they were supposed to be studying (Boiral 1985:47). This lack of interest in—or better still—abdication from 'almost all the major current debates' (Caille 1993:7) in fact made them disciplines which had nothing to do with the future of Africa. And a possible hypothesis is that because they abandoned 'their role as guides and stimulants of the collective conscience charged with voicing the possible and desirable, Africa is still experiencing all sorts of difficulties today' (Caille).

What we are trying to highlight here is the gap between the findings obtained at the time and, by way of consequence, their scant value for the ongoing experience. Our concern here therefore is not to support the inability on the part of the diachronic approach to produce relevant knowledge, as we all know just how important is the anthropological detour in dynamic Africanist anthropology, especially with Balandier (1985) or the importance that Elias (1973; 1974; 1975) attaches to historicity in Giddens' (1987) theory of structuration. Therefore, it is not the diachronic approach that is at fault here, but the way history was used in the analysis and practice of the social sciences in Africa during the first thirty years of independence.

The other practice which attests that the under-development of the social sciences was responsible for the situation of Africa is the support—without the whole some benefit of hindsight—of development strategies adopted by the authorities, especially those of the State-developer. As Mamdani clearly shows, regardless of their stand towards power, whether in government or not, the intelligentsia interested in developmental issues shared the State conception of development and considered the latter as being less the result of a process of bottom-up social trans- formation than the outcome of State initiative (1994:278-82). This gave a stamp of legitimacy to a top-bottom approach whose disastrous results are simply beyond words. Here again, the lack of reflexivity and critical appraisal characterizing this prevailing support of State control as a method of development might be viewed as a cause of the situation in which the continent finds itself today.

The foregoing reveals that an uncritical and un-reflexive practice of the social sciences, combined with a certain implication of the practitioners of the social science, led to an impasse in the delivery of development. The African example is a case in point. Indeed, it shows that 'the conditions making scientific knowledge possible and those of its object are actually one and the same' (Bourdieu 1997:143). Thus, the underdevelopment of the social sciences in Africa is the mirror image of that of African countries. This coincidence/ correspondence of situations or States is thus perceived as evidence that the future of these same countries can also be linked to that of the social sciences in Africa. Moreover, it is in fact because of the political sterility of social science practice on the continent (Caillé 1993:16) that the first attempts of development ended up stalling; the reversal of this trend would augur well for a fresh start (Chabal and Daloz 1999). This looks all the more likely when we know that 'no society has developed economically without the contribution of the social sciences' (Ela 1994:9). It is on this score that the development of the social sciences in Africa can be seen as necessary or holding the key to its future development. However, this twin developed hypothesis does not operate mechanically, because to translate it into concrete reality requires a conducive environment.

Part II

Need for a Conducive Environment: Testing the Twin Developed Hypothesis with Constraints

Our concern in this part will be to prove from the African example that the relationship between the social sciences and development is not automatic. The central theme of our demonstration will be that this relationship is contingent on the emergence of a congenial environment: this refers to the gamut of social/environmental conditions which stand as practitioners determining the efficiency and productivity of the knowledge generated by the social sciences during the development endeavour. Seen from this angle, the question of the relationship of the social sciences with the development of Africa delves into the core of the issue of the social conditions for the opportunity of scientific knowledge mentioned by Bourdieu (1997). This takes us to the socio-logic specific to the social sciences in Africa as well as to that relating to their use on the continent.

Anthropological Study of AIDS

Urgent Need for Reflexive Control of Knowledge Production

To situate the reader, it is necessary to give reasons for the choice of the field of study from which our examples will be drawn. For the socio-logic of the practice of the social sciences, we chose the anthropological field of health which is at the centre of recent topical debates, especially on aspects relating to AIDS. Many reasons can be given for this choice. The first is linked to the scale of this disease in Africa: two-thirds of all HIV-infected persons (25.5 million individuals) live in sub-Saharan Africa (see Eboko 2002:1-2), while the second has to do with the self-examination and questioning to which the

study subjects anthropology (Benoist and Desclaux 1996:365).
More importantly, the examination of the issue of AIDS in
Africa can, all by itself, serve to shed light on the social
conditions for opportunities of scientific knowledge in Africa
because it sits astride action and fundamental research.

The history of how AIDS became anthropologically the
centre of interest of fundamental research in Africa dates back
to the early 1980s, the time the appearance of the first cases
of infection were announced. The pioneer work here was by
Western ethnologists. Arriving on the field, these specialists
on Africa trundled their luggage of observations which had
been tested in their environment—in North America or
Europe. As will be seen later, this had untold consequences.
The notion of groups at risk—social groups identified as being
reservoirs for the virus—was fashionable at the time in the
United States. They spoke of the 4 'Hs'— homosexuals, heroin
users, hemophiliacs and Haitians (Fassin 1996). In explaining
the origins and transmission of the disease, they blamed
inordinate and exotic sexual practices. Clearly, they were
looking for an AIDS-bearing civilization (Paillard 1996:151),
that is, a scapegoat.

This concern is seen in the works of the first foreign
ethnologists carried out in Africa. The team led by Clumeck
(1983) had very much the same aims though not disclosed in
their work. In the interview granted to *Le Monde* newspaper,
Clumeck attributed the disease to the unbridled sexuality of
Africans (*Le Monde* 1987). Other subsequent works made no
bones about attributing the anteriority and no longer the origin
of AIDS to Africa because of the same presupposition. Refer
to the works of Van de Perre and his team (1984) or those of
Serwadda's (1985) team for further conviction.

These early works had a great influence on anthro-pological
research on AIDS in Africa. As Bibeau points out,
anthropologists came to focus on 'cultures of sexuality and

many strove to highlight the diversity, worldwide, of the cultural bases organizing the expression of sexuality. In this area of research... the pitfalls were many and anthropologists did not always succeed in avoiding them' (1996:16).

What is blameworthy in the trend taken by the first anthropological works on AIDS in Africa is not so much the observable transfer of the problem and categories of analysis nor the cultural background of the researchers but the lack of reflexive control over the scientific production that is widely publicised here by renewed fear—that of an unchecked opinion not in tune with the object of research and that of the search for the exotic in order to understand the ongoing reality in one's country (Copans *et al.*, 1971; Copans 1974), fear that facilitated the underdevelopment of the social sciences in Africa and which we must get rid of to pave way for the continent's socio-economic and political development.

Furthermore, it is hard to affirm that the focus on sexual promiscuity in the early works made it possible to better cover all possible fields and to thus enable anthropology to understand the transmission and spread of AIDS on the continent. As Packard and Epstein's study revealed, it prevented the observation of other co-practitioners or indicators which could shed light as much on heterosexual transmission in Africa as on the frequency of sexual contacts (1991). This culminated in 'a narrowing of the field of scientific investigation and hence of opportunities for understanding the disease' (Fassin 1996:8).

It is because anthropologists realized the inherent narrowness of view in this exotic sex approach that the trend in present-day studies has shifted towards reflexive control of the premises for anthropological knowledge on AIDS generated in Africa. This research practice was widely disseminated by the general trend towards deconstructing the categories of analysis received from the initial works. Thus,

Bibeau—who shows that the relevance of anthropological discourse on AIDS depends on the deconstruction of categories linked to the paradigm or rather the 'myth of AIDS-bearing civilization' (Paillard 1996:151) —uses a breakdown of the concept of 'drug culture' to illustrate this and then extrapolates by suggesting that this be done 'in the case of prostitutes, homosexuals, lesbians and their sex partners to show that these groups constitute neither natural categories, homogenous epidemiological entities nor groups allegedly having a single culture' (1996:19). This critical and adjusted look, helping to exert reflexive control on categories summoned to explain reality, is the prerequisite for the development of the social sciences in Africa and, by extension, that of the continent.

An examination of the trend in data collection methods used hitherto points to the same conclusion. At the outset, data was collected using ethnographic methods, but this field tradition was quickly abandoned and gave way to the adoption of the tools of demography or social psychology. The negative effects on the development of anthropological studies are well-known, particularly the restriction to the administration of CAP (competence, attitudes and practices) surveys. The distancing observed today, with the return of the ethnographic tradition, is also a victory in the exercise of reflexive control over the practice and results of research (Fassin 1990, 1995:21-4; also see Bibeau 1996:15), which facilitated greater contributions to knowledge and made it possible for health practitioners to operate more efficiently.

The foregoing is evidence that Africa's future depends on knowledge production founded on strict reflexive control. In fact, it seems that for the social sciences to become an effective tool of development in this part of the global village, they must first begin with their own development. And as we have just shown, this development of the social sciences is contingent on the instituting of a critical reflexive control on knowledge production. The critical reflexivity that we are talking about here is a collective endeavour allowing 'scientific reason to better control itself in and through conflictual cooperation and mutual criticism and to thus gradually free itself completely from constraints and contingencies' (Bourdieu 1997:145). Although the reflexive control of knowledge production may seem easy when viewed in the long-term owing to the cumulative nature of scientific discoveries, the same is not true when it is placed in the short-term.

Detached Engagement: Breaking with the Past

As indicated earlier, the problems confronting the social sciences in Africa in terms of approach are linked to their lack of interest in the present while focusing on the past. Now, not only is 'historical hindsight not necessarily a factor of truth or a condition for the accumulation of data, objectivity or serene discourse' (Sindjoun 1999:3), but especially, as is the case today, the problems bedevilling societies, which the social sciences are striving to understand, run counter to this post-mortem logic according to which things have to cool off before examination begins. In contexts like Africa's where the situation is indeed very urgent, especially at a time when social players are experiencing all sorts of difficulties and have become demanding on account of the urgency of immediacy, can the social sciences deserve their appellation or hope to contribute to development in cases when their interventions only come in afterwards (in laboratories) from a detached standpoint?

In the practice of the social sciences, distance from the object is a prerequisite for their development: this is applicable elsewhere as well as in Africa. Yet, this rule also raises increasing questions when treating the problem of the relationship between the social sciences and the improvement of daily experiences, which exert such stifling pressure. And more than any other domain in the social sciences, anthropological research on AIDS is still confronted by this problem. To be convinced thereof, it suffices to ponder thereon with interest to observe that

> AIDS obliges, as long as the means for attacking the virus head-on remain inadequate, all those who, in various capacities, cooperate in fighting this disease have just one priority—contribute towards the welfare of patients and checking the spread of this pandemic. Solicited to work on this disease more than they have ever been on any other before, anthropologists themselves also have this same obligation (Benoist 1996:5).

This obligation touches on the main difficulty confronting the social sciences in their contribution to development ever since they were empowered as fields of knowledge on man, namely: deconstructing/reconsidering the opposition between commitment and distance (Elias 1993) on which they have thrived. The German sociologist Elias' contribution in this regard is highly instructive in several respects. For purposes of clarity in the text, a presentation of his contribution, though briefly, appears necessary. For Elias, commitment and distance are not opposite poles of behaviour; they reflect extremities of the same continuum (1993:11), but adds that it is distance 'which is the real problem' (1993:11). However, this problem is not without solution, because the two poles are linked by relations of functional interdependence in the sense that the commitment of social scientists 'conditions ... their intelligence of the problems they have to solve as scientists' (Elias 1993:29). But, this requires epistemological vigilance (Grawitz) or, put otherwise, the exercise of critical reflexive control on the frequenting of the two sites. The main significance of Elias' contribution is to have enabled social scientists to formulate a response to 'the pressure exerted in the short-term by social problems which could no longer be solved in the traditional manner and whose solution would require a detour through distance' (1993:25) and a critical reflexive control on its own approach and the knowledge generated.

It is such an Elias-styled solution that the anthropological works on AIDS in Africa re-echo. Fassin has highlighted three main approaches to AIDS anthropology in Africa:

– The first approach achieves a conjunction of proximity, firstly, in relation to action and, secondly, in relation to analysis. Described as applied, it served the cause of the fight against AIDS and adhered to the principle of medical analysis. It had its underpinnings in improved public health through knowledge of the representations and practices surrounding AIDS and everything indicated as risk behaviour.

– The second approach is asymmetrical to the first, inasmuch as it distances itself from action and analysis. This one was described as critical. Though not necessarily indifferent to the fight against AIDS, it questioned the interpretative basis on which the latter was founded, and did not participate concretely in the formulation of programmes.

– The third approach was a combination of the proximity of action and of distance in analysis. Described as implied, it sought to intervene directly in disease-related problems at the level of prevention without necessarily endorsing the presuppositions of health professionals and officials towards whom it adopted a more or less distanced attitude.

These three approaches to the real in the field of AIDS intelligence prove that the study of present issues does not in any way foil the relevance of works conducted with seriousness and self-control. It also shows that interest in present issues allows for significant contributions to the resolution of urgent daily problems. Practice is constantly undergoing adjustment in step with contributions of research to a better knowledge of AIDS. Although arriving after the fact can guarantee greater distance from the object of research and perhaps better analyses, it cannot in any way justify the attitude of shying away from urgent daily problems which would be tantamount to burying one's head in the sand. This means that the development of the social sciences and that of Africa necessitate a clean break with a certain way of conducting research which has hitherto required that interest in a reality be awakened only when it has become history. An approach based on distanced participation in the study and resolution of present problems is therefore relevant and recommended. This seems all the more relevant because we know the social to be essentially dynamic and unpredictable (Balandier 1981) and hence, hard to confine to models built from other social dynamics. Our intention here is not to argue that diachronic studies contribute nothing to the betterment of the living conditions of the populations or to understanding of real phenomena, but to bring out the limitations and consequences of an approach based exclusively on the diachronic factor without taking account of the daily experiences of Africans.

The evolution of AIDS anthropology in Africa also conveys other lessons, linked to the origin of researchers who are active in this field of study. This takes the discussion into the constraints of distancing. As we have seen, the mistakes made at the outset stemmed from the fact that scientific practice was undertaken without preliminary testing of the applicability of the categories of observation and analysis imported into Africa. This seems to suggest that the fact of not being a native would not guarantee the quality of research results; hence, the importance of involving African researchers—researchers well schooled in the art of unearthing the secrets of daily rites and local socio-cultural symbols. However, while such involvement is desirable and probably important, it would be unreal to believe that familiarity with an object of study would guarantee the ability to better grasp it than an Africanist from another cultural sphere. It should be said that the refinement of anthropological views on AIDS in Africa is more the work of Africanists than African researchers. The development of the social sciences in Africa and, by extension, the relevance of their contribution to guaranteeing stable livelihoods and the take-off of the continent may also come from a practice of research which prioritizes the contribution of combined teams of locals and Africanists, that is, players familiar with the research setting as well as researchers alien to that environment.

Yet, does it suffice to work energetically to produce relevant knowledge in the hope of sparking off development in Africa? In other words, does the development of the social sciences in and by itself suffice to trigger that of the continent? This question takes us back to the issue of the use and value of the knowledge generated in this area.

The Imperative Use of the Social Sciences

Need for an Intelligentsia and Society Linkage

We do not use 'intellectuals' here to refer to the African intellectual in its broadest sense, but have limited ourselves to specialists in the social sciences—sociologists, anthropologists, jurists, political scientists, economists, etc. The reader will have an impression of repetition here, but our intention is more to show that among the conditions of feasibility of the twin developed hypothesis, there is the exigency of the emergence of a responsible intelligentsia who are conversant with the stakes of the moment and their obligations towards society. Therefore, analysis here is not driven by the question of the scientific competence of African researchers, but the ability of the latter to listen to the people they are supposed to study.

The hypothesis thus considered is that the intellectual has a responsibility—one of the most crucial—for the onward march of history and the progress of the nation. When Plato suggested that the philosopher be king, he was referring to such a responsibility. The author of *The Republic* considers that the philosopher—understood as an intellectual—must be in charge of administering the city because, through his ability to access the intelligible world, he alone can do Good understood as the beautiful, the just and the true (Chatelet 1965). According to Plato, the 'practice of the Good' is the essential prerequisite for being able to rule the city with fairness and justice: 'all will work for the best in a city if one who knows Good, the philosopher, is king' (Auroux and Weil 191:383).

This role that Plato confers on the intellectual is not a given, especially in Marxist analyses. Gramsci, for example, believes that intellectuals are 'functionaries of superstructures', meaning, technicians at the service of the dominant group. Thus, their role in the management of public affairs cannot be direct, inasmuch as it is publicized by these institutions which they serve as organic intellectuals (1983). The responsibility ascribed here to the intellectual is 'to organize social hegemony and State domination' (Ramsis Farah 1994:290) and to give it legitimacy through the production and reproduction of knowledge (Poulantzas 1980:5). In this perspective, the intellectual's role will be less managerial than instrumental or ideological. To properly discharge it, he opposes the civil society, perceived as the place in which is exerted the ideological and political domination of the State, name given to the dominant class (Abé 2001:230).

However, it is hard to accept this definition of the intellectual's role because it is at variance with what is observed every day in the social domain and especially because it encourages the intellectual's disconnection from society. Two arguments may be raised here. From the point of view of relations with social groups, the African intellectual cuts across many classes: 'intellectuals belong to no class in particular. They find themselves on various rungs of the class system' (Ramsis Farah 1994:292) and hence, at the service of both the State and the civil society. Moreover, Sartre states, 'the most direct enemy of the intellectual is [what could be called] ... the fake intellectual ... whom Nizan named the watch dog, summoned by the dominant class to defend their particular ideology with purportedly strict arguments presented as the outcome of exact methods' (1972:53). He is fake on two counts: firstly because he fails to use the one thing which makes him an intellectual, his critical faculties, accepting to legitimize the practices of the players instead of pondering them in order to discover the truth they contain; and secondly, because he has lost touch with reality, especially with all real problems in the social field. Now, in essence, his position 'forces him to be committed to all the conflicts of our time' (Sartre 1972:58) and the challenges confronting the society, through knowledge production. One of Africa's current challenges is in the management of public affairs, which in itself depends on the mastery of ways and means leading to development, that is, through better knowledge of obstacles and prospects.

Indeed, as Sartre points out, one 'needs to know the world to change it', to transform it and to make it better (1972:68). This shows that the intellectual is not only one who thinks but also one who acts and whose thoughts carry weight and authority in charting the course of life for the city. And it on the strength of his responsibility towards society that the intellectual owes it to himself to help the latter adopt solid landmarks so as 'to find a common base, transcending the struggles tearing individuals apart, the ignorance which makes individuals get carried away by opinions and appearances, and an incomprehensible multiplicity of beings, events, thoughts and languages' (Eboussi Boulaga 1993:27). Here is where the intellectual has a 'directing and organizing' function (Mbata B. Mangu 2003:3) in the management of the city and more broadly, in the under-development of the African continent, a duty that obliges him to connect to society if he wants to succeed in achieving what will be in line with the objectives it is pursuing.

But it seems in Africa, researchers in the social sciences had their own peculiar and rather curious perception and understanding of the intellectual's responsibility in the management of public affairs. It would be interesting to do a comparative study by holding up their behaviour during implementation of the political liberalization processes against the aspirations of African societies.

At the start of the 1990s, events literally zoomed by on the social and political fronts. After many years of 'forced silence' (Conac 1993:6), the people of sub-Saharan Africa regained their sense of political initiative which had been stifled for a long time. This renewed initiative was reflected in near-permanent and noisy street demonstrations in Yaounde, Libreville, Niamey, Dakar and Abidjan. Anger (Monga 1994) was vented through social movements that challenged the established order and restored the people's lost dignity (Bourgi 1990:63). A social ingenuity was displayed at the time which strongly affirmed the determination of African societies to have their own back on the State (Bayart 1992; also read Woods 1992). What these social movements conveyed was the people's will to break from 'a political past dominated by one-party regimes, fraught with violence and bloodshed' (Galloy and Gruenais 1997:12). They also expressed their rejection of a method of governance which was based on falsehood, wheeling and dealing, corruption and arbitrariness.

However, the people's militancy for profound political change received only negligible support from the intelligentsia, especially social scientists. Barring a few isolated cases of intellectuals who threw in their support for these social movements, an assessment of how the conduct of these knowledge-producing players affected African societies compels us to recognize the defeat of thought (Finkielkraut 1987) and its proponents. With 'the splintering of political space by multi-party politics' and its corollary— the reappearance of people falling back on tribal identities— a return to corporatism was noted among the social science researchers (Diouf 1993:44-5), that is, a betrayal of the people who looked up to them for guidance.

Another category preferred to be on the side of the dictator in power. As Mbata B. Mangu aptly points out, 'there are indeed, many examples of individual [African] intellectuals who cooperated with and continue to serve dictatorial regimes for their selfish material and financial survival and who helped to usher in or consolidate dictatorship instead of democracy' (2003:20). The example of the Nigerian political scientists who served the military dictatorship of General Ibrahim Badamasi Babangida is still fresh in our minds (Ibrahim 1997:114-17). They were used each time to justify and legitimize the refusal of political liberalization for which Nigerians were, however, clamouring through mass demonstrations. In Cameroon, we all know the role played by such jurists and political scientists as A. Kontchou Kouomegni, J. Owona, Bipoum Woum etc... appointed at the time as cabinet ministers to give the regime in power a customized constitution and electoral law to enable it stay in power or to preserve the status quo.

Such examples are not isolated cases, even as the betrayal of the social sciences must not be understood as being attributable only to jurists and political scientists (Mbata B. Mangu 2003:20). The case of Côte d'Ivoire is a good illustration of the gross instrumentalization of the social sciences. On the pretext of doing scientific work, reality was

over-stretched in order to give a stamp of legitimacy to a
particular ideology. Those we meet here are researchers who
produce pseudo-knowledge brandished as justification for the
ethnic cleansing underway in the country. It is on the basis of
these so-called scientific works that social scientists succeeded
in devising a classification which had, on one side, Ivorians—
those who are allegedly indigenes—and on the other,
impostors—those whose parents allegedly came from a
neighbouring country. It is here that the concept of Ivoirité
(the fact of being an Ivorian) took its instrumental value. This
concept, visibly used to legitimize the disqualification of some
members of the political elite from running for office today, is
a recent invention by some of the country's historians such as
Niagnon Bouah, Laurent Gbagbo and Henriette Diabate. We
see the same treachery in those intellectuals who sought to
trade their pens for elective or ministerial positions. When
their plans failed, some were not content with turning their
backs on the amphitheatres or the avenues of research, but
actually threw in their lot with armed rebellions. Witness the
former Zaire where Ernest Wamba-Dia-Wamba turned into
a military leader in the ranks of the rebellion in South Kivu
Province.

The intellectual abroad is another case of such betrayal.
Many researchers in the social sciences indeed went on
voluntary exile to escape from the harsh local realities,
especially in 'search for greener pastures' (Tapsoba 2000:30),
thus abandoning the people to their fate in the battlefield for
the future establishment of democracy and the rule of law.
We do not fail to recognize the work of a good many
intellectuals to establish democracy on the continent,
sometimes paying with their lives. What we are saying here is
that this category represents an insignificant percentage
compared to the other category—those who threw in the towel.
Similarly, we are not denying that some intellectuals left their

countries, fleeing from the wrath of repressive structures put in place by autocratic systems to maintain order and discipline within the social corps. Our concern here is to highlight the category that preferred exile to carrying on the struggle, even though in amphitheatres among students, at a time when the latter were prepared to clash with autocratic regimes and help usher in the rule of law and democracy.

Since democracy today is a viable alternative for the development of Africa (Mappa 1995), the disconnection between the African intelligentsia and society stands as an obstacle to the continent's take-off: hence, 'the urgent need to break from the isolation that has always been the lot of lecturers and researchers in Africa—social isolation in relating with society' (Diouf 1993:47). One of the major constraints besetting the African development scene which replicates that of the social sciences is linked to the utilization and value of the results of research carried out in this area.

Development through the Social Sciences

Although the disconnection mentioned above is visibly the work of social scientists, it would be hard to limit oneself there without appearing partial and somewhat partisan. Indeed, the fact that their practitioners use it as a means of betraying social activists by thwarting their legitimate aspirations must not cause us to lose sight of their marginalization—marginalization at both national and international.

Nationally, such marginalization mostly comes from State bodies, even though one cannot fail to note that relations between social scientists and civil society are not always the best. It is indeed hard in most African countries to talk of a policy for the furtherance and development of the social sciences.

Speaking of Senegal, Coulon observes that the social sciences are in relative neglect (1992:3) while Bierschenk and

Mongbo remark that 'Benin has, for long, remained almost fallow in terms of knowledge in the social sciences' (1995:54). Motaze Akam highlights a similar observation in the case of Cameroon (1994). Further, he brings out the disparity between instruments instituting research in the social sciences in this country and the actual practice of research, concluding that 'political authorities in Cameroon consider research in the social sciences and its practitioners as white elephants' (1994:78). These three countries are not isolated cases, as the same observation could indeed be made elsewhere. This shows that African States share a disregard for the furtherance of the social sciences.

Disdain for this area of knowledge leads to its marginalization in the conduct of public affairs. The nature of the relations its practitioners have with the authorities is self-explanatory in several respects. Cameroon is a case in point. As testified by Motaze Akam, in Cameroon, as in all the other African countries, public authorities should be the prime beneficiaries of the expertise of social science practitioners—in ministries, public and semi-public corporations:

> The sociologist or anthropologist is perceived in a conflictual light by techno-bureaucrats. This conflict-ridden perception is explained by the fact that the latter see the work of researchers as mere speculation or pretexts (sic), even claiming to know better than them. This, because such techno-bureaucrats perceive research as useless work since, to their mind, everybody can undertake it (1994:7).

The foregoing reveals that the expertise of social science researchers is given scant attention by public authorities. Put differently, it is not utilized because of its negative bias. This is true of both its utilization and the results of its investigations, which are attended by many problems, primarily linked to their publication (Motaze Akam 1994:76). Another reason is the poor dissemination of such scientific works: it was far easier during the one-party era, for example, to obtain a publication for Americans, French or Dutch than for nationals to obtain a social science journal or work published in the very same town in which they lived.

This lack of development of knowledge generated by the social sciences also has social aspects. Civil society such as non-governmental organizations often vie with social scientists in playing the role of researchers when they are not obliged to make their cumbersome presence felt during the implementation of development projects.

At the level of international organizations and external funding bodies, the place of the social sciences is no different. German Technical Cooperation Agency (GTZ) illustrates and gives us an example of the situation. Marginalization here has two main aspects: apart from the fact that GTZ has no consistent policy on the use of and recourse to the social sciences, it rarely relies on social scientists. Out of 2,800 employees, only about 4 percent are social scientists (Foster 1994:83).

It emerges from the foregoing that there is 'insufficient transfer of the results of the expertise' (Foster 1994:84) of the social sciences at national and international levels. Thus, regardless of relevance of the practice of the social sciences in Africa or that of the results of research conducted by social scientists, it is still difficult to jump-start development of this continent. In other words, its situation cannot match the level attained by these disciplines. Hence, it is urgent to forge a synergy between social scientists and those who are supposed to use the knowledge they produce.

Conclusion: Enhancing Cooperation and Institutional Development

In this paper, we set out to examine the relations between the social sciences and the development of Africa. Our reflection was structured in two parts around the twin developed hypothesis. This was accompanied by a cautions link to the structuring of a concept specific to the construction of the social science academy. We showed in the first part that the situation of multi-faceted crises in Africa may be perceived as the consequence of the under-developed practice of the social sciences on the continent. Based on the situational coincidence and the historical constant that no society has developed economically without the contribution of the social sciences, we established that social sciences are necessary for Africa's development. Yet, this development cannot operate mechanically or in the manner of Pavlov and his dog.

The second part of our paper enabled us to establish that the effectiveness of the social sciences is conditioned by a conducive environment whose constraints are scientific and linked to social experience, especially in the relations that practitioners have with the object of their study and the users of their expertise. In fact, the emergence of an enabling environment depends on the reflexive development of the practice of the social sciences in Africa and on that of their use. Ultimately, all these must enhance cooperation between the fields of research and of development practitioners. As Foster points out,

> This means that development practitioners must become better acquainted with the social field and understand the rationality of its expertise. On the other side, the 'providers' of this expertise are required to further adapt to the require- ments for the implementation of development, while pre- serving their own rationality and critical faculties (1994:86).

This means that organizations such as CODESRIA engaged in the work of developing the social sciences in Africa still have a long way to go. The example of CODESRIA is unique in Africa for now, and there is no doubt about its investments as well as its potential to face the present-day challenge.

However, at a time when there is increasing talk of African integration, has this institution the necessary funds for its own development through the creation of sub-regional branches which will bring it closer to researchers and the realities on the continent? In our view, it would appear that this type of institution is central to the challenges that the anomic situation of Africa poses to the social sciences today. That is why we have chosen to conclude with a question: What is CODESRIA's future as it celebrates its thirtieth anniversary?

Notes

1. We allude to this notion here because it sheds light on the paradox of the global village which highlights two trends that, though apparently contradictory, are in reality related to one another: globalisation and the search for local identities. The reflections in this paper revolve around the said paradox.
2. The reader could also consult J. Copans' inventory on Africanist studies and, in particular, those carried out by the African Studies Association and those published in the *Annual Review of Anthropology* (1990:396-398).
3. The notion of the global village does not refer here to its current usage which entails the idea of collectively rehabilitating displaced populations in zones that are not yet inhabited. It is used here to designate the process whereby the world is transformed into a global village.

Bibliography

Abé, C., 2001, 'L'Afrique à l'épreuve de la mondialisation', *Cahier de l'ucac*, 6, Yaoundé.

Abé, C., 2001a, 'Problématique de la société civile en Afrique: la contribution de la sociologie de l'entrecroisement des civilisations', *Bastidiana*, 33-34, jan-juin.

Adarelegbé, A., 1991, 'University and Administration under Military Rule', in A. O. Sanda (ed.) *Understanding Higher Educational Administration in Nigeria*, Ibadan: Fact Finders International.

Aguessy, H., 1982, 'Infrastructure et politique des sciences sociales: le cas du Bénin', in Mbonigaba Mugaruka, et al (eds.) *Sciences sociales en*

Afrique, s. l., études du CERDAS, nov.

Amin, S., 1985, *La déconnexion*, Paris: La Découverte, coll. 'Cahiers libres (413)'.

Amin, S., 1989, *La faillite du développement en Afrique et dans le tiers monde*, Paris: L'Harmattan.

Auroux, S. et Weil, Y., 1991, *Dictionnaire des auteurs et des thèmes de la philosophie*, Paris: Hachette.

Bakary, Tessy D., 1992, 'L'État en Côte d'Ivoire. Entre dépendance et autonomie relative', Université de Laval, Laboratoire d'études politiques et administratives, juin.

Balandier, G., 1981, *Sens et puissance*, Paris: Puf, coll.,'Quadrige', 3e édition.

Balandier, G., 1981, *Sociologie actuelle de l'Afrique noire*, Paris: Puf, coll. 'Quadrige'

Balandier, G., 1985, *Le détour. Pouvoir et modernité*, Paris: Fayard.

Bayart, J.-F., et al., 1999, *La criminalisation de l'État en Afrique*, Bruxelles: éd. Complexes.

Bayart, J. -F., 1985, *L'État au Cameroun*, Paris: Presses de la Fondation nationale des sciences politiques, 2e édition.

Bayart, J.-F., 1989, *L'État en Afrique (La politique du ventre)*, Paris: Fayard.

Bayart, J.-F., 1992, 'La revanche des sociétés africaines', in J.-F. Bayart et al. *La politique par le bas en Afrique noire*, Paris: Karthala.

Bayart, J.-F., 1999, 'L'Afrique dans le monde: une histoire d'extraversion', *Critique internationale*, 5, automne.

Benda, J., 1965, *La trahison des clercs*, Paris: J. J. Pauvert.

Benoist, J. et Desclaux, A., 1996, 'Pour une anthropologie impliquée', in J. Benoist and A. Desclaux (eds.) *Anthropologie et sida. Bilan et perspectives*, Paris: Karthala.

Benoist, J., 1996, 'Introduction. Le sida entre biologie, clinique et culture' in J. Benoist and A. Desclaux (eds.) *Anthropologie et sida. Bilan et perspectives*, Paris: Karthala.

Bénot, Y., 1995, *Massacres coloniaux*, Paris: La découverte.

Bibeau, G., 1996, 'La spécificité de la recherche anthropologique sur le Sida', in J. Benoist and A. Desclaux (eds.) *Anthropologie et sida. Bilan et perspectives*, Paris: Karthala.

Bidima, J.-G., 2000, 'Le corps, la cour et l'espace public', *Politique africaine*, 77, mars.

Bierschenk, T. et Mongbo, R., 'La recherche en sciences sociales au Dahomey et au Bénin depuis les années 1970: l'hégémonie du paradigme développementiste', *Bulletin de l'APAD*, 10.

Boiral, P., 1985, 'Logiques de la recherche et logiques d'action', in P. Boiral, J.-F. Lanteri et J. -P. O. de Sardan *Paysans, experts et chercheurs en Afrique*.

Sciences sociales et développement rural, Paris: CIFACE/Karthala.

Bourdieu, P., 1997, *Méditations pascaliennes*, Paris: Seuil.

Bourdieu, P. and Wacquant, J. D. L., 1992, *Réponses. Pour une anthropologie réflexive*, Paris: Seuil.

Bourgi, A. et Casteran, C., 1991, *Le printemps de l'Afrique*, Paris: Hachette.

Bourgi, A.: 1990, 'L'Afrique: le réveil de la démocratie', *Afrique 2000*, 1, Avril-Juin.

Brunet-Jailly and Rougemont, A. (éd.), 1989, *La santé en pays tropicaux*, Paris: Doin

Caillé, A., 1993, *La démission des clercs: La crise des sciences sociales et l'oubli du politique*, Paris: La Découverte.

Chabal, P. and Daloz, J.-P., 1999, Africa Works. The Political Instrumentalization of Disorder, Bloomington & Oxford: James Currey and Indiana University in association with LAI.

Chanlat, J. -F., 1998, *Sciences sociales et management*, Paris: éd. Escka.

Châtelet, F., 1965, Platon, Paris: Gallimard.

Clumeck, N., et al., 1984, 'Acquired Immunodeficiency Syndrome in African Patients', *New England Journal of Medicine*, Vol. 310, 8.

Conac, G., 1993, 'Introduction', in G. Conac (ed.), *L'Afrique en transition vers le pluralisme politique*, Paris: Economica.

Conac, G., 1993, 'Les processus de démocratisation en Afrique', in G. Conac (ed.), *L'Afrique en transition vers le pluralisme politique*, Paris: Economica.

Copans, J., 1974, *Critiques et politiques de l'anthropologie*, Paris: F. Maspero.

Copans, J., 1990, *La longue marche de la modernité africaine*, Paris: Karthala.

Copans, J., 2000, 'Les sciences sociales africaines ont-elles une âme de philosophie ? ou du fosterage de la philosophie', *Politique africaine*, 77, mars.

Copans, J.et al., 1971, *L'anthropologie: science des sociétés primitives?* Paris: Denoël.

Coquery-Vidrovitch, C., 1985, *Afrique noire. Permanences et ruptures*, Paris: Payot (2e éd., Paris: l'Harmattan, 1993).

Coquery-Vidrovitch, C., 1999, *L'Afrique et les Africains au XIXe siècle. Mutations, révolutions, crises*, Paris: Armand Colin.

Coquery-Vidrovitch, C., (éd.), 1988, *Processus d'urbanisation en Afrique*, Paris: L'Harmattan.

Corcuff, Ph., 1995, *Les nouvelles sociologies*, Paris: Nathan.

Coster (de), M., 1999, *Sociologie du travail et gestion des ressources humaines*, Bruxelles: De Boeck Université, 3e éd.

Crozier, M., 2000, *A quoi sert la sociologie des organisations*, 2 tomes, Paris: éd. Seli Arslan.

74   The Social Sciences and Africa's Future

Diaw, A., 1994, *Démocratisation et logiques identitaires en acte. L'invention de la politique en Afrique*, Dakar: CODESRIA.

Diouf, M., 1982, 'Infrastructure et politique des sciences sociales au Sénégal', in Mbonigaba Mugaruka, et al (eds.) *Sciences sociales en Afrique*, s. l., études du CERDAS, nov.

Diouf, M., 1993, 'Les intellectuels africains face à l'entreprise démocratique: entre citoyenneté et expertise', *Politique africaine*, 51, oct.

Diouf, M., 1998, 'La société civile en Afrique: histoire et actualité. Notes provisoires', communication, 9e Assemblée générale du CODESRIA, Dakar (Sénégal), déc.

Dumont, R., 1962, *L'Afrique noire est mal partie*, Paris: Seuil.

Dumont, R., 1982, *L'Afrique étranglée: Zambie, Tanzanie, Sénégal, Côte d'Ivoire, Guinée Bissau, Cap Vert*, Paris: Seuil, coll.

Durkheim, E., 1986, *De la division du travail social*, Paris: Puf, coll.

Drucker, P., 1990, *The New York Realities*, New York, Harper and Row Publishers.

Eboko, F., 2002, 'Sida, sociétés et politiques en Afrique: un nouveau défi pour la science politique', communication, séminaire méthodologique international organisé par la section camerounaise de l'AAPS, Yaoundé (Cameroun), 21-26 janv.

Eboussi Boulaga, F., 1993, 'L'intellectuel exotique', *Politique africaine*, 51, oct.

Ekoué Amaïzo, Y., 2001, 'PMA ou PFI ? Les pays faiblement industrialisés: la globalisation par défaut', *Le courrier ACP/UE*, 186, mai-juin, 'Pays les moins avancés'.

Ela, J.-M., 1990, *Quand l'État pénètre en brousse...Les ripostes paysannes à la crise*, Paris: Karthala.

Ela, J.-M., 1994, *Restituer l'histoire aux sociétés africaines. Promouvoir les sciences sociales en Afrique noire*, Paris: L'Harmattan.

Ela, J.-M., 1998, 'Refus du développement ou échec de l'occidentalisation? Les voies de l'afro-renaissance', *Le Monde diplomatique*, oct.

Elias, N., 1973, *La civilisation des mœurs*, Paris: Calmann-Lévi.

Elias, N., 1974, *La société de cour*, Paris: Clamann-Lévi.

Elias, N., 1975, *La dynamique de l'Occident*, Paris: Clamann-Lévi.

Elias, N., 1993, *Engagement et distanciation. Contributions à la sociologie de la connaissance*, Paris: Fayard, traduit de l'allemand par Michèle Hulin.

Elias, N., 1997, 'Towards a Theory of Social Processes: A Translation', *The British Journal of Sociology*, Vol. 48, 3, sept.

Etounga-Manguelle, D., 1993, *L'Afrique a-t-elle besoin d'un programme d'ajustement culturel ?* Paris: éditions nouvelles.

Etounga-Manguelle, D., 1995, 'Culture et développement: ou les conséquences d'une modernisation tardive de nos schémas sociaux', *Terroirs* (revue africaine de sciences sociales), 002, jan.

Fall, B. (éd.), 1997, *Ajustement structurel et emploi au Sénégal*, Dakar, CODESRIA.

Fassin, D., 1990, 'La démarche de la recherche', in D. Fassin et Y. Jaffré (éds.), *Sociétés, développement et santé*, Paris: Ellipses.

Fassin, D., 1995, 'Du commentaire considéré comme tauromachie. A propos d'enquêtes CACP et de réseaux VIH', Transcriptase, 41.

Fassin, D., 1996, 'L'anthropologie, entre engagement et distanciation. Essai de sociologie des recherches en sciences sociales sur le sida en Afrique', paper presented during the international symposium on 'Sciences sociales et sida en Afrique', Sali, 4-8 November.

Finkielkraut, A., 1987, *La défaite de la pensée*, Paris: Gallimard.

Fogui, J.-P., 1990, *L'intégration politique au Cameroun. Une analyse centre-périphérie*, Paris: LGDJ, coll. 'Bibliothèque africaine et malgache'.

Foster, R., 1994, 'L'expertise en sciences sociales et la coopération technique-Quelques réflexions sur la relation délicate lors des 3e journées de l'APAD à Bamako', *Bulletin de l'APAD*, 10.

Friedmann, J. et Sandercock, L., 1995, 'Les dépossédés', *Le Courrier de l'UNESCO*, mars, 'Le développement pour qui' ?

Giddens, A., 1987, *La constitution de la société*, Paris: Puf, coll. 'Sociologies', translated from English by M. Audet, 2e éd.

Giri, J., 1985, *L'Afrique en panne*, Paris: Karthala.

Gramsci, A., 1983, *Selections from the Prison Notebooks*, New York, International Publishers, 7e Impression.

Grawitz, M., 2001, *Méthodes des sciences sociales*, Paris: Dalloz, coll. 'Précis Dalloz', 11e édition.

Grignon, C., 2002, 'Sociologie, expertise et critique sociale', in Lahire, B. (éd.), *A quoi sert la sociologie ?*, Paris: La Découverte, coll. 'Textes à l'appui/laboratoire de sciences sociales'.

Guillaume, H., 1998, *La technologie et l'innovation*, Paris: La documentation française.

Hugon, Ph., 1993, 'Les effets des politiques d'ajustement sur les structures politiques africaines', in G. Conac (ed.), *L'Afrique en transition vers le pluralisme politique*, Paris: Economica.

Hugon, Ph., 2000, 'Prospective de l'Afrique subsaharienne', *Futuribles*, 257, oct.

Ibrahim, J., 1997, 'Political Scientists and Subversion of Democracy in Africa', in G. Nzongola-Ntalaja and M. Lee (eds.) *The State and Democracy in Africa*, Harare, AAPS Books.

Jackson, W., 2000, 'Mondialisation, exode des compétences et développement des capacités', in S. J. M. Tapsoba (ed), *Exode des compétences et développement des capacités/Brain Drain and Capacity Building in Africa*, s.l., ECA/CRDI/OIM.

Jaffré, Y. et. De Sardan, J.-P. O (dir.), 1999, *La construction sociale des maladies*, Paris: Puf, coll. 'Les champs de la santé'.

Kabou, A., 1991, *Et si l'Afrique refusait le développement ?*, Paris: L'Harmattan.

Kamto, M., 1987, *Pouvoir et droit en Afrique noire*, Paris: LGDJ, coll. 'Bibliothèque africaine et malgache'.

Ki-Zerbo, J., 1992, 'Le développement clés en tête', in J. Ki-Zerbo (éd.) *La natte des autres. Pour un développement endogène en Afrique*, Dakar: CODESRIA.

Kobou, G., 1999, 'Ajustement structurel et exclusion sociale: une analyse fondée sur le marché du travail', in L. Sindjoun (éd.) *La révolution passive au Cameroun. État, société et changement*, Dakar; CODESRIA.

Kom, A., 1993, 'Intellectuels africains et enjeux de la démocratie: misère, répression et exil', *Politique africaine*, 51, oct.

Lahire, B., 2002, 'Utilité: entre sociologie expérimentale et sociologie sociale', in B. Lahire (éd.) *A quoi sert la sociologie ?*, Paris: La Découverte, coll. 'Textes à l'appui/laboratoire de sciences sociales'.

L'homme et la société, 1999, *Revue internationale de recherches et de synthèses en sciences sociales 'Politiques des sciences sociales'*, n°131, L'Harmattan.

Le Pensec, L. (éd.), 1988, *Vingt questions sur l'Afrique: des socialistes répondent*, Paris: L'Harmattan.

Leymarie, Ph., 1994, 'La Somalie, nation éclatée', *Manière de voir*, 21, fév., 'le désordre des nations'.

Loovoet, B., 1996, 'Guinée: Les tentations du passé. Eléments d'analyse de la scène politique', *L'Afrique politique*, Paris: Karthala.

Mahieu, R., 1990, *Les fondements de la crise économique en Afrique*, Paris: l'Harmattan.

Mamdani, M., 1994, 'L'intelligentsia, l'État et les mouvements sociaux en Afrique', in M. Diouf et M. Mamdani (éds) *Liberté académique en Afrique*, Dakar: CODESRIA.

Mappa, S. (éd.), 1995, *Développer par la démocratie ? L'Afrique subsaharienne sous les injonctions occidentales*, Paris: Karthala/forum de Delphes.

Mbata B. Mangu, A., 2003, 'Contribution des intellectuels congolais au mouvement nationaliste, à la lutte pour l'indépendance et la démocratie au Congo-Kinshasa', communication à la conférence continentale du 30e anniversaire du CODESRIA, Dakar, 10-12 déc.

Mbembe, A., 1985, *Les jeunes et l'ordre politique en Afrique*, Paris: L'Harmattan.

Mbembe, A., 1999, *Du gouvernement privé indirect*, Dakar, CODESRIA.

Mbembe, A., 2000, *De la postcolonie*, Paris: Karthala.

Mbonigaba Mugaruka et al. (éds.), 1982, *Sciences sociales en Afrique*, s. l., études du CERDAS, nov.

Médard, J.-F., 1983, 'La spécificité des pouvoirs africains', *Pouvoirs*, 25, 'Pouvoirs africains'.

Médard, J.-F., 1986, 'Public Corruption in Africa: A Comparative Perspective', *Corruption and Reform*, Vol. 1, 2.

Médard, J.-F., 1994, 'Politics from above, Politics from below', communication on The NFU Conference: State and Locality, Oslo, June 18-20.

Médard, J.-F., 1998, 'La crise de l'État néo-patrimonial et l'évolution de la corruption en Afrique sub-saharienne', *Mondes en développement*, t. 26, 102.

Monga, C., 1994, *Anthropologie de la colère: société civile et démocratisation en Afrique*, Paris: l'Harmattan.

Motazé Akam, 1994, 'Le marché de l'expertise et la place du socio-anthropologue: le chercheur en sciences sociales en Afrique', *Bulletin de l'APAD*, 7, juillet, 'Les sciences sociales et l'expertise en développement'.

Ndoumbé-Manga, S. and Atem Endaman, 1982, 'Infrastructures et politiques des sciences sociales au Cameroun', in Mbonigaba Mugaruka, et al (eds.) *Sciences sociales en Afrique*, s. l., études du CERDAS, nov.

Nnoli, O., 1993, *Deadend to Nigerian Development. An Investigation on the Social Economic and Political Crisis*, Dakar: CODESRIA.

Northoff, E., 1993, 'La crise africaine et l'impact des sciences et des technologies', in *Le courrier ACP/CE*, 139, mai-juin, 'les facteurs du développement'.

OCDE, 1986, *La politique d'innovation en France*, Paris: OCDE.

Ochwada, H., 1994, 'Les intellectuels au Kenya et les crises des études africaines', *Bulletin du CODESRIA*, 4.

Onitri, H. M. A., 1990, 'Le développement de l'Afrique dans les années 1990: des perspectives pour une décennie d'espoir', *Afrique 2000*, 1, avril-juin.

Packard, R. M. et Epstein, P., 1991, 'Epidemiologists, social scientists and the structure of medical research on AIDS in Africa', *Social Science and Medicine*, Fall 33, 7.

Paillard, B., 1996, 'Le mythe de la civilisation sidatogène', in J. Benoist and A. Desclaux (eds.) *Anthropologie et sida. Bilan et perspectives*, Paris: Karthala.

Poulantzas, N., 1980, *State Power Socialism*, London, Verso.

Prunier, G., 'Rwanda: histoire vraie de fausses ethnies', in H. Lelièvre (éd.) *Demain l'Afrique: le cauchemar ou l'espoir*, Bruxelles: Ed. Complexes, coll. ' interventions'.

Ramsis Farah, N., 1994, 'Société civile et liberté de recherche en Egypte', in M. Diouf and M. Mamdani (éds) *Liberté académique en Afrique*, Dakar: CODESRIA.

Requier-Desjardins, D., 1972, *Le Congo au temps des grandes compagnies concessionnaires, 1899-1930*, Paris-La Haye: Mouton.

Scarrit, J.-R. and Mozzafar, S., 1999, 'The Specification of Ethnic Cleavages and Ethnopolitical Groups for Analysis of Democratic Competition in Contemporary Africa', *Nationalism and Ethnic Politics*, Vol. 5, 1, Springs.

Serwada, S., et al., 1985, 'Slim disease: A New Disease in Uganda and Its Association with HTLV-III infection', *Lancet*, ii.

Simon, P.-J., 1999, 'Sociologie et réforme sociale', *Sciences humaines* (revue), 25, juin-juil, 'A quoi servent les sciences humaines'.

Sindjoun, L., 1999, *Science politique réflexive et savoirs sur les pratiques politiques en Afrique noire*, Dakar: CODESRIA.

Sindzingre, N., 1983, 'L'interprétation de l'infortune: un itinéraire senufo (Côte-d'Ivoire)', *Sciences sociales et santé*, Vol. I, 3-4.

Tapsoba, S. J. M. et al (eds.), 2000, 'Brain Drain and Capacity Building in Africa', joint publication of the Economic Commission for Africa, the International Development Research Centre, and the International Organization for Migration.

Tshikala, K. Biaya, 2000, *Les jeunes, la violence et la rue à Kinshasa. Entendre, comprendre, d'écrire*, Dakar: CODESRIA.

Weber, M., 1959, *Le savant et le politique*, Paris: Plon.

Wieviorka, M. (dir.), 1998, *Raison et conviction: l'engagement*, Paris: Textuel.

Wieviorka, M., 2000, 'Sociologie postclassique ou déclin de la sociologie?', *Cahiers internationaux de sociologie*, Vol. CVIII, janvier-juin, 'Sociologies inactuelles, sociologies actuelles ?'

Woods, D., 1992, 'Civil Society in Europe and Africa: Limiting State Power through Public Sphere', *African Studies Review*, Vol. 35, 2, sept.

The Social Sciences: A Necessity for the Future of Africa? Africa Needs Her Promise

Mildred Kiconco Barya

Introduction

This essay discusses the necessity of social sciences for the future through the behavioural science tool embedded in social psychology. It attempts to integrate concepts, theories, and the results of empirical studies from the various disciplines of cultural anthropology, economics, political science, sociology, social work and social welfare, in understanding, predicting, and directing change. The behavioural approach explores and reflects in detail our knowledge of theoretical and policy debates, whose impact depends on the utilisation of the social science research in creating the future of Africa that we want.

Background to the Social Sciences: A necessity for the Future of Africa

There are three types of future: the possible, the probable, and the preferred. According to the World Bank Group Report 2003, 2.8 million people, more than half of the people in developing countries, live on less than $2 a day; 1.2 billion people are wallowing in poverty and earn less than $1 a day. About 840 million people are going hungry and 40 million are living with HIV/AIDS, Africa being the worst affected part of the world, with an estimated 23 million infected. In Uganda alone, 35 percent of the population are the core poor, nearly 50 percent lack clean drinking water, over one million are living with HIV/AIDS, there are two million AIDS orphans, 134 children out of every 1,000 born alive do not live to celebrate their fifth birthday, and over 1.2 million people are displaced by the 17 year-old conflict in the Northern region of the country.

To change the situation, the World Bank uses its financial resources to meet millennium development goals: eradicate extreme poverty and hunger, achieve universal primary education, promote gender equality and empower women, reduce child mortality, improve maternal health, combat HIV/AIDS, malaria, and other diseases, ensure environmental sustainability and develop a global partnership for development by 2015.

To apply a behavioural change tool embedded in the social science theories especially social psychology, meeting goals requires that policies be set right, based on a thorough understanding of people's behaviours; orientation, motivations, the trends that shape their values, and the perceptions that mould their actions. This requires new goal framing; emphasising strengths as Africa's needs motivators, rather than negative events, because ideally, what you focus on grows. The IMF admits that it is failing in Africa.

The contribution of the Social Sciences for the future has been ignored because social scientists are primarily not trained and legitimised to do action research, compared to the natural scientists, who are licensed by society for their sustainable models of change. Behavioural approaches help integrate basic and applied social science research, thus moving from being strictly theoretical and descriptive to being more prescriptive about the future.

Ignoring the importance of behavioural concepts and the need to set policy right will result in policy deficiencies, frustrations, failure to attain goals, thus making us permanent beggars and hostages, instead of us creating a future that is Africa's promise.

Policies and programmes designed to effect change and improve the quality of life in Africa are not set right to empower communities on the sound understanding of behaviour and strengths of populations, gleaned from the knowledge of social science theories. This results in the misinterpretation of policies, distortions, focus on negative actions, breakdown of African values and the failure to create a future that we want.

This essay aims to demonstrate how behavioural approaches rooted in social science theory and research provide a framework in which policy goals can be formulated, based on the understanding of orientation, values and motivations/ needs of populations in order to empower and create ownership that facilitates positive actions and lead to goal attainment (desired future).

Discussion

Orientation

Behaviour is basically goal oriented. For people to be able to do something different from what they were able to do before requires a change in behaviour. Most policies aimed at changing bad situations to better ones rely on the accounting approach. The accounting system identifies directly who pays what and who receives from what, when assessing the impact of a policy. Actual numbers of those benefiting from immediate results can be obtained from quantitative analyses in evaluations.

For example, the United Nations High Commissioner for Refugees (UNHCR) supported schools and schemes show 9,223 children enrolled in preschool education, 52,620 in primary education, 5,380 in secondary education, 377 in formal vocational skills training, 314 in teacher training and 71 in university education. Until June 2002, UNHCR also assisted 1,074 persons through its literacy programmes, supported 85 refugee primary schools, 1,175 primary teachers, 118 secondary teachers, and focused on building the capacity of 34 national secondary schools in Uganda.

The accounting approach alone is limited in the sense that it lists numbers of those benefiting from the programme, and judging the direct impact. A behavioural orientation, however, establishes the right value of a free public service by observing the indirect effects of a policy. For example, where there is universal primary education, parents may decide to send their children to school to take advantage of free school lunches.

Again, offering free public education in a village means more to a household that was initially sending its children to a school 10 km away from the village, than to a household whose children were initially not enrolled. Public expenditures can be effective in reducing poverty only when the policy setting is right. It is hardly worth increasing spending on primary education for girls if distortions in labour markets still prevent female school graduates from securing employment.

For instance, Uganda's target to eliminate gender disparity at secondary education level is still unfavourable to girls, with a 55:45 ratio in favour of boys. Factors including inappropriate sanitation, social and cultural biases hinder the achievement of this goal.

It is futile to increase spending on agricultural extension or research if overvalued exchange rates make agricultural activity unprofitable. Pro-poor expenditures must be accompanied by pro-poor policies. This is hardly the case at this time. Simply spending money on the provision of a service without attending to the efficiency with which that spending generates services, and to the direct and indirect impact on the intended beneficiaries cannot be recommended (Filmer, Hammer, and Pritchett 1998).

Wrong indicators like increased production can be taken for the success of policy implementation, while at the export market rate the exchange is not profitable to the farmer. One of the false indicators is the improved lives of farmers, who have been taught new farming techniques that have increased production dramatically. But then they realise that due to free market conditions, the country receives the 'same' imports and this causes price reductions and floating of home products, thus a loss to farmers who become poorer than before, while the policy evaluation boasts of improved farming services.

In the year 2000, Ugandan surveys showed that more than 90 percent of the money earmarked for schools actually reached them, with improved payment procedures, and information exchange with stakeholders. The scrapping of school fees for primary schools following the government policy of Universal Primary Education (UPE) pushed school enrolment figures from 3.4 million in 1996 to 7.3 million in 2002. This is a half-baked, and false indicator of success since its measure does not go all the way to consider the 'same' students who become frustrated after graduation, when they realise they cannot be employed anywhere, and that their peers who never went far in school are seemingly better off as regards their needs fulfilment.

Besides, the high population growth rate has not resulted into a proportional improvement in the pupil–teacher ratio.

The government is aiming at achieving a 100 percent enrolment into primary school by 2015, but the Uganda country progress reports indicate that the quality of education might be sacrificed to quantity. The accumulation and acquisition of human capital rather than human resources cannot be interpreted as development if more educated people cannot find avenues where to practice and exchange their knowledge.

In addition, some of the millennium development goals' shortcomings are a result of policies not set right. They focus on the negative picture, and that results in the negative being magnified rather than overcome. There is no policy in Africa that concentrates on utilising the wealth of the nation, say our human resources, and other areas in which we can be encouraged to excel. It is true that emphasising the negative and weaknesses of Africa cripples hope, rather than providing the needed incentive for change.

Little wonder therefore that by the end of 1998 figures released by UNAIDS showed that over 34 million people were infected with the AIDS virus world-wide, with the subsequent statistics released surpassing the previous ones. Initially the epicentre of the epidemic was the inter-lacustrine part of central and Eastern Africa. The highest levels of HIV infection now appear to have occurred in the southern and western parts of Africa: Botswana, Malawi, South Africa, Zambia, Zimbabwe, Côte d'Ivoire, Ghana and Nigeria.

For example, pregnant women in one urban centre in Botswana have HIV prevalence rates of 48 percent. Some surveillance sites in Zimbabwe showed rates between 20 and 50 percent among pregnant women tested anonymously. South Africa has estimated that 3.6 million South Africans are now living with HIV/AIDS.

These prevalence statistics paint a frightening future for the continent. The extended family system that used to be regarded as essentially African has virtually ceased to exist as a safety net of support for kin. Life expectancy plunges to levels lower than those of the past. In Botswana, projections show that with 25 percent of adults infected with HIV/AIDS, the life expectancy of their children will be around 41 years by the year 2005. Projections further show that prevalence rates of 10 percent will cause life expectancy to drop by as much as 17 years.

Under the millennium development goal of eradicating poverty and extreme hunger by 2017, between 1997 and 2000 poverty levels have increased from 60 to 66 percent in Uganda, and the continued conflicts in the northern regions continue to undermine gains in other areas, with an estimated 1.2 million people displaced as a result of rebel activities in the region.

The target to reduce infant mortality by two-thirds in children below five years by 2015, records the rate on the increase. Between 1995 and 2000, infant mortality rates shot up from 81 to 88 per 1000 live births, undermining the government's target of reducing this to 78 per 1000 births in 2002.

We can alter such future scenarios that most African countries face today, by reframing the goals to accentuate our strengths and political commitment towards change. To illustrate this with a classroom example, students who are constantly told that their mathematics grades are poor and in need of improvement may be consumed by that fact and end up failing other subjects as well, for the maths situation is magnified before them by the teacher. On the other hand, if the teacher highlights those dimensions in which the students excel, that may cover up for the maths failures, and even reinforce the students with brighter perspectives to altering their behaviour. When policy and goal framing are set right, orientation leads to shaping values and motivation.

Shaping values

Shaping values is an outcome of orientation. Values stem from understanding who we are and what we stand for, thus informing our attitudes concerning relevant issues. Recent studies of civil society, NGOs and ideology, reveal that issues of values and philosophy do not appear to be of any interest to the majority of respondents. This is a rather grave situation. Without a commonality around these attributes, how is an alternative model of development shaped and advocated?

Looking at the future through the eyes of political science, research on Africa has focused for many years on the failed state syndrome in Africa. State systems in Africa were copied from western values and models that were not politically, culturally and socially embedded in Africa. They corresponded neither to African tradition, nor African views of modernity in a rapidly changing globalised system. Since no African seriously believes in a stateless society, the only solution is to rebuild the state by taking African realities into account (Trefon et al, 2002).

By understanding our value system as Africans, we can know how to interpret concepts like governance. The late Mwalimu Nyerere argued that governance is a concept applied by aid givers to aid seekers in an arrogant and patronising manner. He used to argue that one of the objectives of improving governance of our countries is to strengthen the African state and thus enable it to serve the people of Africa better. How do we achieve this if we do not use social science research in reflecting on our value system? If we do not incorporate various social science disciplines into understanding our worth, how will we know our strength that enables us to serve the people of Africa?

Human functioning is always situated in a context. It involves the shared symbols of a community, its traditions and tool-kit, passed on from generation to generation and constituting the larger culture. The process of change therefore is not straightforward. Social scientists can negotiate transformative change successfully, by providing knowledge of the role played by values in understanding why certain recommendations made in the past have not been acted upon, as well as why those which have been adopted as policy are frequently not followed.

Besides the values of populations, our own attitudes concerning the value of social science discipline, its power as an applied science and its worth as a basis for dealing with human problems, affect the confidence with which behavioural change is practised.

The concept of values at the same level with motivation leads to empowerment

Motivation

The motivation of people depends on the strength of their motives. Motives are sometimes defined as needs, wants, drives, or impulses within the individual. Motives are directed toward goals, which may be conscious or unconscious. Motives therefore are the whys of behaviour. They arouse and maintain activity and determine the general direction of the behaviour of an individual or group. In essence, motives or needs are the mainsprings of action.

All the policies to change the future of Africa for the better are motivated by negative events and statistics. There is a big difference in asking: how do we have more food, to how do we end poverty? The latter amounts to nothing while the former motivates in the right direction. Visually, it is hard to work towards reducing poverty. Framed positively, it is easier to work towards making riches/wealth. Reducing mortality rates is nothing. But working on those factors related to cultural practices, traditional attitudes that affect sexuality and health yields greater results.

The negative framing of goals results in avoidance behaviour and creates a diversion that makes us concentrate on symptoms rather than the actual disease. They emphasise where we are weak and in that way makes us weaker, more vulnerable to defeat. It is essential to note that goals can only be attained if they are 'rightly' motivated. Without awareness and without learning the right motivations, there will be policy misinterpretations and deficiencies.

For example, parents may be motivated to send their children to school simply because policy says so, education is free, or the country is pursuing low literacy levels. These are wrong motivators. However, if people learn that by going to school they will be able to engage in gainful employment, contribute to individual, household and national development because of the resource that they are, and lead a quality life, those would be the right motivation to yield greater, planned results.

This is also true about eradication of HIV/AIDS, malaria and other diseases. What should make people abstain from sexual activities or lead them to adopt the use of preservatives? Would it be limited to the fear of dying? The fear of death works for only a short while but not to bring about a lifetime behavioural change. Avoidance behaviour has its limits and it is no wonder that despite the HIV/AIDS rates having fallen to 6.1 percent in 2000, they rose to 6.5 percent in 2001.

Malaria is yet to be fought. Several interventions including abolishing taxes on mosquito nets, home-based fever management, free pre-packaged malaria treatment for children—all these do not work unless populations are taught to understand why they should live, or continue to live. By learning that they have a legacy for the motherland, that they have a big role to play in the development of Africa, by being told that they have the potential to be world changers, only then can they begin to pursue her promise, to value life and thus fight to live.

Goal framing aside, Hersey et al., (1993) suggest that motives or needs are the reasons underlying behaviour. People have hundreds of needs that compete for their behaviour. What then determines which of these motives a person will attempt to satisfy through activity? The need with the greatest strength at a particular moment leads to activity, while satisfied needs, or needs blocked from being satisfied decrease in strength, people are not motivated to seek goals to satisfy them.

Goals should be set high enough so that we stretch to reach them, but low enough so that they can be attained. The practice of 'dangling the carrot just beyond the donkey's reach,' is not a good motivational device. Blocked motives, and continually unsuccessful avoidance behaviour, may lead to forms of irrational coping behaviours. The blocking or thwarting of goal attainment is referred to as frustration. Frustration may increase to the extent that the individual engages in aggressive behaviour, rationalisations, regression, fixation and resignation. Frustrated people tend to give up constructive attempts at solving their problems, and will continue to exhibit the same behavioural pattern over and over again, although experience has shown that it can accomplish nothing. Frustration can freeze old and habitual responses and prevent the use of new and more effective ones. Maier has shown that although habits are normally broken when they bring no satisfaction or lead to punishment, a fixation actually becomes stronger under these circumstances. Resignation occurs when people lose the hope of accomplishing their goals in a particular situation and withdraw from reality and the source of their frustration. Activities from high-strength needs result in goal directed activity and goal activity; concepts that are important to practitioners in understanding human behaviour.

Two other important factors that affect need strength are expectancy and availability. Expectancy tends to affect motives, or needs, based on past experience, and availability tends to affect the perception of goals, and reflects the perceived limitations of the environment. It is determined by how accessible the goals that can satisfy a given need are perceived to be by an individual.

An example of how perception can affect behaviour was dramatically illustrated in an experiment with a fish. A pike was placed in an aquarium with many minnows swimming around it. After the fish became accustomed to the plentiful supply of food, a sheet of glass was placed between the pike and the minnows. When the pike became hungry, it tried to reach the minnows, but continually hit its head on the glass. At first, the strength of the need for food increased and the pike tried harder than ever to get to the minnows. Finally, its repeated failure at goal attainment resulted in enough frustration that the fish no longer attempted to reach the minnows. When the glass partition was finally removed, the minnows again swam all around the pike, but no further goal directed activity took place. Eventually, the pike died of starvation while in the midst of plenty of food. In both cases, the fish operated according to the way it perceived reality and not on the basis of reality itself.

Individuals act on the basis of their perceptions or interpretation of reality and not on the basis of reality itself. One of the reasons that we study the behavioural sciences is that they give us ways of tuning our perceptions closer and closer to reality. The closer we get our perceptions to a given reality, the higher the probability that we can have some impact on that particular piece of reality.

According to the message from the UN General Secretary Kofi Annan, marking the UN World Day, serving humanity wherever its needs are greatest, helping the peoples of the world find common solutions to common problems are the main plans. Africa's need is not to find common solutions to common problems. Our need is how to focus on the positive aspects that we have as a nation, what we can do, and do it better. It is necessary to make this shift, so that the current behaviour of receiving policies formulated by others, the current status quo of thinking that we are too poor because statistics say so, the current culture that is led to believe that the World Bank Group is genuinely interested in helping us... can come to an end. Only then will we be able to transform for the better, and effect changes in the international system. Our realised capabilities will then equip us to handle the problems we face without fear of shaping wrongly, motivating wrongly. Right motivation leads to empowerment.

Empowerment

Empowerment helps us concretise on what we are best at, without being taken advantage of. The moment we realise that we are not skilled at certain games, then we will not join the playfield because we will know that we are bound to lose. Millennium development goal number eight focuses on developing a global partnership for development. The most recent happening under this goal in Uganda is the Africa Growth Opportunities Act (AGOA), which started recently. Uganda opened its investment door to Sri-Lankan investors, who began operating an Apparels Tri-Star factory. The company makes garments from Uganda's cotton and exports to the US. It recruited about 1,400 young girls selected from various parts of the country.

However, on 24 October 2003, Apparels Tri-Star fired around 265 girls (without paying their dues, benefits, and repatriation costs) despite a court order secured by the employees and trade unionists restraining the action. The workers protested against poor working conditions, sexual harassment, mistreatment and poor pay. Their salary was shs80,000 per month ($40), lunch consisted of a doughnut and water, they shared dormitories with men, each girl was supposed to make 100 garments in an hour, and they were working 13 hours without extra pay (*The Monitor Newspaper*, 26 October 2003). The presidential advisor on AGOA revealed that Tri-Star was receiving about $40 million a week from its exports. The senior presidential advisor on AGOA saw the AGOA case as poor management of human resources. On 27 October 2003, *The Monitor Newspaper* released a news article revealing that government contributed Shs5.4 billion to the investors, provided free factory premises, and on management's behalf even carried out the recruitment of the girls from several districts on. Why we had to do this is both a mystery and misery. Why we even had to think of exporting the garments by the exploitation of our human resources, when our own people are going naked for want of clothing is something I am yet to understand. We have a ready market at home. If we cannot handle export investments, have value for our human resources, and ensure that investors respect the employment laws that govern our land, why should we get into such business at all? Why should we facilitate our own exploitation in the name of global partnership? If in implementing policies we are not empowered to plan, question, and realise when we are trading Africa's strength for a second enslavement, we will continually fail to achieve what is best for the future that we want. What is economic growth at the expense of human life, human rights, and human dignity? In other African countries, the import of foreign systems unsuitable to the background of the country has had very adverse effects. Anything that is transplanted from anywhere else must be only what has been proven appropriate in the local conditions.

Since most development takes place with the people themselves taking an active part, the human factor will have to be both inspired and well equipped so that they can play an effective role in their own development. For this they must develop full confidence in themselves. Their minds and hearts must be full of this new enthusiasm to work for the development of their country. With the recognition of the worth and dignity of every individual, only then can we make the best and positive use of opportunities for our development. Somalia has began to recognise that optimum use of the human factor, when directed towards the goal of development, will transform Somalia into a country vibrating with human enthusiasm which will speed up the developmental process.

Empowerment enables us to value our resources in all dimensions, and leads to the concept of ownership.

Ownership

People participate in the change process because they have been empowered to understand that the transformation belongs to them, they can own it, they can possess it. This provides an environment that allows continual realignment of goals and an opportunity for growth and development. Research indicates that commitment increases when people are involved in their own goal setting. If people are involved, they will tend to engage in much more goal directed activity before they become frustrated and give up.

In management, an important step in becoming more effective in fostering responsible behaviour is determining whether that behaviour is acceptable or unacceptable, and then answering the question of who owns the problem in terms of behaviour identified. The concepts behind the ownership of problems applies to any setting in which a 'leader' is trying to influence the behaviour of others. Gordon's concept of 'who owns the problem' can be combined with William Oncken's helpful 'monkey-on-the-back' analogy. Blanchard, Oncken and Burrows define a monkey as the 'next move' on the path to solving a problem. When a manager agrees to 'think about' a follower's problem, then ownership of the next move shifts from the follower to the manager. Before the shift, responsibility for the action was on the follower. After the shift, when the manager takes ownership of the monkey, two responsibilities are assumed: responsibility for the problem, and responsibility for updating the follower on the progress of the problem. The manager will not make much progress on the monkey because it is buried under all of the other monkeys accumulated from other followers. This is what happens when the World Bank and other donor agencies continue to own Africa's monkey. Responsibility shifts from us to the policy makers. With owning our own monkeys, we will feel the responsibility to take positive action towards building Africa's promise.

What stops us from owning our monkeys is that we are not setting our own policies. If we were doing so, then we would fully participate and be more committed to change. We would be involved in policy formulation and implementation not because it is a government initiative but because it is our own venture, and this would result in positive actions.

Positive action

Positive action includes actions that totally liberate the nation towards achieving desired goals. This concept of positive action can be best understood through the analogy of the popular Chinese saying: World Bank policies are not teaching developing countries how to 'fish' based on, they are simply giving out fish, following statistics they have captured in their reports.

It is a shame that with all the rich and fertile soils that Africa has, agricultural products, minerals, people... we can still go 'hungry' because at the heart of it, we are a society that is not aware of itself. The human condition is not apparent, and we do not see the denied or unrecognised social opportunities that can generate new agendas for the future and change the current image.

In 1965, Singapore had the same GDP as Uganda. The prime minister of Singapore channelled people's behaviours towards those actions that were positive and now, Singapore ranks among the highly developed nations. Uganda to this present day focuses on failures, weaknesses, foreign donations, and the future is dreaded. Recognising positive actions on which we can 'feed' ourselves, uncork our stores, leads to goal attainment.

Goal Attainment

Goal attainment is the predicted variable at the end of change process. Billy Rojas suggests that 'The future doesn't just happen; we make it and we can use it'. Looking into our own human condition using the eyes of social science behavioural theories, setting our own goals on the understanding of our values and motivations, will contribute towards our empowerment to own the change process and engage in positive actions in which our goals can be attained. Thus, it means succeeding in making the future that we want, and fulfilling Africa's promise, because, she needs it, and we owe it to her.

Conclusion

Social science concepts offer rigorous insights into human behaviour, and increase the level of awareness or consciousness of reality reflected in social issues. Africa is currently living in a traumatised state. Social science research has its contribution to make towards healing the wounds. In Sweden, independent basic research has a high status, which is emphasised by the annual award of the Nobel Prize to outstanding researchers. This has made Sweden one of the world's countries that invest most in research as a necessity to understand ourselves and the world we live in. Social science research constructs interactive methods that have increased awareness about the importance of changing behaviour.

References

Agence France Press, 2003, 'IMF admits it is failing in Africa', 24 October.

Biesheuvel, S., 1987, 'Psychology: Science and Politics. Theoretical Developments and Applications in a Plural Society', *South African Journal of Psychology*.

Blanchard, K. et al., 1989, *The One Minute Manager Meets the Monkey*, New York: Morrow.

Bourguignon, F., et al., 2003, *The Impact of Economic Policies on Poverty and Income Distribution*, New York: World Bank and Oxford University Press.

British Psychological Society, 1998, 'The Future of the Psychological Sciences: A Report Prepared for the Scientific Affairs Board by the Working Party on the Future of the Psychological Sciences'.

Festinger, L., 1957, *A Theory of Cognitive Dissonance*, Stanford, California: Stanford University Press.

Gordon, T., 1984, *Leader Effectiveness Training*, New York: Bantam.

Hersey, P. et al., 1993, 'Motivation and Behaviour', in *Management of Organisational Behaviour: Utilising Human Resources*, New Jersey: Prentice-Hall, Inc.

Mafeje, A., 2001, 'The Impact of Social Sciences on Development and Democracy: A Positivist Illusion', address given during the National Research Foundation's President's Awards event.

Maier, Norman R.F., 1961, *Frustration: The Study of Behavior Without a Goal*, Ann Arbor: The University of Michigan Press.

Robert, W. N., 1976, *Behavioral Intervention: Contemporary Strategies*, New York: Garden Press.

Ruhela, S, P., 1993, *The Preferred Future for Somalia*, New Delhi: Vikas Publishing House.

Toure, D., 2003, 'Despite the Gains, the Journey Ahead Remains a Long and Trying One', *The Monitor Newspaper,* Kampala, on UN Day.

Trefon, T. et al., 2002, 'State Failure in the Congo: Perceptions and Realities', *Review of African Political Economy.*

UNAIDS, 1998, A *Measure of Success in Uganda: The Value of Monitoring Both HIV Prevalence and Sexual Behaviour*, UNAIDS Case Study.

United Nations, 2003, 'Message from the UN General Secretary marking UN Day', UN Day supplement, Kampala, *The New Vision Newspaper.*

Wallerstein, I., 1999, *The End of the World as we Know it: Social Science for the 21st Century*, Minneapolis: University of Minnesota Press.

World Bank Publications available online: http://www.worldbank.org/publications.

Yamba, B., AIDS *Research in the Social Sciences: What Have We Learned in the Last Decade?* News from Nordic Africa Institute.

Development Concerns in Africa: The Value of an Ethnographic Approach

Esther van Heerden

Introduction

Since their inception in the early modern age, the status of the social sciences—broadly defined as those academic disciplines that involve themselves in the study of humankind—have been an issue of contestation (Mouton and Muller 1997) on a number of levels. Dismissed by some as 'soft sciences' i.e. having little concrete scientific value, a lot of effort has gone into establishing their relation to the natural sciences; either as sciences in themselves (Kellner 2003; Turner and Roth 2003) or by outlining their unique strengths and describing how their orientation, subject matter and method(s) differ from those of the so-called natural sciences (Gordon 1991; Bohman 1991).

At a time when social science researchers in Africa, are beleaguered by 'isolation and scientific marginalisation, precarious material conditions, political repression, a debilitating brain drain and lack of academic freedom' among other factors. (see www.codesria.org), the value of social knowledge for the future of the continent is questioned anew. Diminishing state support and funding for research projects in many African countries has led to a greater demand for effective research that offers practical solutions to pressing social problems.

In addition to the conventional criteria for evaluating social research, namely validity and reliability (Chambers 1985:17), the ability to illustrate the relevance and significance of research that can be made publicly available has become more crucial. But how does one determine relevance? And what are the most pressing concerns for Africa? Some (see George et al. 2000) characterise these concerns as the 'rise of new forms of colonialism, imperialism, domination and social oppression', but even these terms are applied in such a vague way that they might be taken to refer to a number of different problems. In order to keep the paper specific I therefore want to focus on the contentious issue of development in Africa which, in some sectors, is believed to be a 'new' form of social oppression by the industrialised West. I will therefore commence by sketching the background to development in Africa, and locating discourses of development within a larger framework of social science research; showing how development knowledge has been deconstructed in the post-positivist epoch.

An Impoverished Africa: Development as Cure

According to the Report of the Independent Commission on Population and Quality of Life (1996:14), there are areas in Africa which are among the world's poorest; 'they have the lowest quality of life and the most regrettable situation for women'. Social research has shown how malnutrition, ill health, lack of educational opportunities, chronic unemployment and limited or no access to vital services in less developed areas perpetuate a cycle of poverty (see Taylor and Mackenzie 1992). Often it is women that suffer the most. Poverty—'the battle of our time' as this Report puts it—is therefore perceived to be the central enemy, for which 'development' is the antidote (Wangoola 2000). The push for economic development in Africa began during the struggle for independence and the subsequent decolonisation process (Fruzzetti and Ostor 1990:15). Most early development discourse had close links with modernist notions of linear progress. It was widely believed that through economic reform and increased production African countries would achieve an economic growth rate at par with that of the industrialised nations; the benefits of which would eventually trickle down to the rest of society. Ironically, development strategies narrowly defined in terms of economic growth have often only succeeded in exacerbating existing problems. Today, Africa's debt service ratios remain high, the quality of life for the majority of Africa's inhabitants has declined in both absolute and relative terms (Taylor 1992: 215), environmental degradation persists, disparities among social classes are widening in many societies as a result of current developmental policy (Mackenzie 1992:7), populations are on the increase, institutional and physical infrastructure remain inadequate, etc.

One reason for the failures is that the development recommendations of institutions such as the World Bank, the IMF and WTO and the prescribed structural adjustment programmes are often inappropriate and do not take the diversity of African contexts into account. Moreover, national and local sovereignty is eroded in countries due to an excessive reliance on external funding and expertise, rather than development driven by grassroots initiatives—initiatives for which local people can take a measure of responsibility. An acute recognition of the failures of many development projects has coincided with a postmodern turn in the social sciences. Although the three major aspects of the social scientific enterprise—theory, data collection and data analysis (Babby

1998:24)—have remained relatively constant, the interrogation of social knowledge prompted by postmodern theorising raises a plethora of definitional, moral and power concerns that are linked to processes of knowledge production. For those social researchers involved with development, crucial questions for consideration include: what constitutes social knowledge about development? Whose knowledge claims are privileged? Who is serviced by such knowledge? How is social knowledge structured and represented? Despite these challenging questions for which there are no straightforward answers, it is my conviction that the social science disciplines, and social research specifically, are indeed a necessity for the future of Africa. By introducing the social sciences as dynamic, maturing disciplines and outlining the shift from positivism to a more auto-critical and deconstructive theorising below, I intend to show that the postmodern critique does not necessarily render social knowledge irrelevant; rather it has forced social scientists, specifically those working as development practitioners, to become more attuned to a constantly changing, hybrid 'Africa'.

Positivism and Beyond: The Social Sciences in Transition

Although my intention here is not to map the history of the social sciences, I want briefly to illustrate how the framing of their conceptual scope is historically situated. Social science paradigms, ranging from Social Darwinism to Symbolic Interactionism, Structural Functionalism and Role Theory, come into pre-eminence and later fall by the wayside, only to be revived again in a new guise. Whereas the dominant development paradigms between the 1950s and the 1970s put forward a technocratic model of technological transfer from the 'West' to Africa, the utilisation of local resources and accounting for the social impact of development policies have become more important in later years. However, there has not been absolute break between past and present beliefs. For example the early development discourse called modernisation theory, despite being criticised for its simplistic, ahistorical and ethnocentric underpinnings, is still influential (Gardner and Lewis 1996:12). Social science vocabulary is also continuously recompiled as certain concepts gain social currency whilst other formerly legitimate ones are discarded. The conceptualisation of 'culture' as encompassing 'all the skills and characteristics human beings acquire as members of a society' (Wicker 1997:31), which has often been employed in development discourse, encouraged thinking of so-called cultures in terms of bounded, homogenous totalities. This enabled cross-cultural comparisons and the formulation of grand theories. Gradually such notions of culture have been superseded by more flexible conceptions that accommodate the elusiveness and ambiguity inherent in the term 'culture' that makes it so difficult to define. As Fay (1996:61) points out: 'cultures are inherently polyglot, conflictual, changeable, and open'—qualities that are not easily accommodated by rigid developmental policies. Nowadays most concepts have been problematised to such an extent that social scientists in my experience often write or 'speak' in inverted commas as a way of safeguarding themselves against accusations that they are insufficiently aware of the multiple meanings underlying the terms of their discussion. The concept of development is one such an example that is to be used only with the 'inverted commas of the deconstructed 1990s' (Gardner and Lewis 1996:1).

Also with regard to social science research methods, what was once considered as the essentials in research manuals has changed. In the modern era for example, methodological debates mostly centred on how to erect a value-free science in order to uncover so-called true, universal facts. Positivism advocated the erection of explanatory research frames that could offer seemingly complete and coherent answers to complex human phenomena. In this regard the power relations between respectively a clinical researcher (often male, heterosexual and of European descent) closely engaging with 'subjects' were seen as stable, unitary categories unilaterally fixed. The researcher was cast in the dominating role and expected to remain distanced, objective and rational at all phases of the research project. Especially in Africa research relations were intrinsically unequal, even a 'colonial' relation (see Harding 2003) since the researched were allotted little say in the research process. Ironically, as Harding (2003:299) points out, the 'subjects', who often stemmed from a disadvantaged group, were further disempowered by research intended on managing those under the control of bureaucratic state structures. Michel Foucault for one proclaimed that mainstream social science is a weapon bent on normalising its subjects (Fay 1996:200). The discomfort arising from this ascribed ideal research conduct in terms of so-called neutral and objective conduct seeps through in many research textbooks that almost fanatically provide guidelines on how to construct and pre-test questionnaires in a way that limits interview bias and reactivity as much as possible.

According to textbook prescriptions (see Bernard 1988; Babbie 1998) survey research questions which have often been deployed in developmental research, should be unambiguous, well-planned; understandable; concise; both exhaustive and exclusive; avoid double-barrelled and emotive questions etc. Consistency of respondents' statements over time is taken as one of the most important measures of a report's reliability. All these measures are an attempt to control the factors 'external' to the research process in order to obtain 'scientific' data that are statistically valid and easily comparable. Clearly I am simplifying research practices for the sake of my argument. While I am by no means denying the importance of careful thinking about the conduct of research, such as the construction of questionnaires which is often helpful in developmental research, it is increasingly recognised within social science domains that social theorising in itself is inevitably located within specific contexts, supported by particular ideologies and framed by value-driven ideals. In fact, social theorising and the practice of research has always been historically specific with distinct moral and political dimensions (Mouton and Muller 1997:3). Moreover researchers are increasingly required to consider their own multifaceted identity construction within socio-economic, academic, historic etc., milieus (Collier 125). The concept of development for example has been accused by some as being embedded in neo-colonial constructions of the world and a key ideological tool in global power relations (Gardner and Lewis 1996:1).

Epistemologically the debates about social scientific theorisation and research conduct thus shifted as social sciences moved from the positivist epoch to being more attuned to modern day realities, partly in response to the postmodern critique that challenged the very foundations of positivist science. The notion of so-called value free social theorising removed from local contexts has been virtually abandoned in favour of a more 'hands-on' engagement with social issues. As Jeremy MacClancy (2002:110) writes, it is increasingly acceptable for social researchers, and anthropologists specifically, to become involved with local issues such as 'monitor[ing] compliance with codes of human rights... and [helping] to establish channels through which abused indigenous peoples can make effective protests...' Given this background I want to sketch the implications of such a paradigm shift to developmental concerns in Africa.

Enlightenment and Empowerment Redefined—
Implications for Development

'Where the old logic of the social sciences sought unity, the new logic finds complexity; where the old logic sought idealised reconstructions, the new logic begins from the actual practices...' (Bohman 1991:7). Enlightenment, empowerment and emancipation have guided the modernist social theories. The notion of a critical social theory as 'the catalytic agent in the overthrow of a given social order' (Fay 1987:28) with classical Marxism as a good example, has come under attack, mainly because of the emphasis on an ultimate truth that will set people free and the limits on the ability of critical science to engender social change (Fay 1987:206). But the three E's, as Mouton and Muller (1997:5) call them, are still influential in shaping social science research agendas. Certainly many theorists (see Fay 1996) support the notion of a critical theorising with the distinct goal of guiding people towards a greater knowledge of the mechanisms underlying the dominant social orders. Less radical postmodern scholars are often primarily concerned with exploitation, power discrepancies, empowerment, and the 'development of rhetorical tools to deconstruct and critique linguistically constructed and textually mediated social realities and provide alternative interpretations of texts' (Collier 123).

Thus, although social science aims of truth and enlightenment set forth by dogmas such as empiricism and positivism have been problematised by a recognition of the indeterminacy of social phenomena, they clearly have not been lost (Kellner 2003:255) in the sense that the production of knowledge is still valued. There seems to be a general consensus that research, as a social activity, should be carried out for the benefit of society, and specifically Africa (see Prah 1993; Abrahams 1997). Despite the questioning of knowledge and the diversity in the range of research that is carried out, a common unifying theme remains empowerment. Of course, empowerment is defined differently within the social sciences depending on the particular research orientation. Advocates of multi-culturalism for example envision *empowerment* as the 'struggle for a freer and more flexible formation of groups and identities based on self-consciously shared values, orientations, activities and politico-economic positions' (Turner 1994:424). Many health researchers and activists on Aids want to *empower* people to make wise choices given the correct information on the disease in an effort to slow the transmission of HIV. The many variations of feminism including liberal, Marxist and psychoanalytic feminism, are all fixated on different means of *empowering* women whether through the safeguarding of individual rights by the state; changing the class structure and providing equal opportunities to genders or by exploring the depths of the female psyche. In development rhetoric one view of empowerment states that ordinary people need to be enabled to 'take charge of their lives, to make communities more responsible for their [own] development, and to make governments listen to their people' (Mackenzie 1992:26)—a mission statement which again raises the disconcerting questions of validity, relevance and value as to the diverse roles that the social sciences, specifically with regard to development research, should play.

According to Prah (1993:12) social science research does not have a good track record when it comes to maximising public interest: 'At the level of scientific research expertise capable of producing researched insights for policy and technological innovations... in the experience of Africa as whole, since the onset of the era of independence in the late fifties... such expertise has made a relative meagre impact on transforming the African earth for the betterment of the human condition'. While assessing Prah's argument falls beyond the scope of this paper, the social sciences have had to strengthen the links between policy and practice and increasingly social researchers find themselves working in applied research contexts. Especially with regard to development, social scientific methods are increasingly being used to develop grassroots development and relief: assessing local needs, establishing effective mechanisms so that assistance reaches the most needy, and ensuring that community development programmes are equitable and sustainable (De Waal 2002:252).

In the remaining part of the paper I will illustrate how ethnography, a research method conventionally associated with the practice of anthropology, can be a valuable research tool. It can be utilised to yield research insights that can contribute to the generation of development research that enlighten and empower both researcher and researched through among other things, an attention to context, by being people-centred and situating the 'local' within the 'global'.

Ethnography: A hands-on Approach

As a research method gaining currency in nearly all the disciplines of social science (Chambers 1985:174), but conventionally associated with the discipline of anthropology, the increasingly widespread application of ethnography is a testimony to the increasing multi-disciplinary trend in social science research. Ethnography nowadays can be characterised in varied ways including multi-vocal (see Grillo 1997), multi-sited (see MacClancy 2002), global (see Burawoy 2000) or comparative ethnography (see Gingrich and Fox 2002). Core elements of the method include direct exposure to research settings over an extended period of time; intensive, action-based researcher immersion in daily lives which among other things entails living like the 'locals' and an open-minded approach to lived experience which ideally means taking little for granted.

But like any other social method, ethnography has not been uniformly understood by all its practitioners. This is aptly illustrated by Michael Burawoy's outline of the divergent approaches that the Chicago and Manchester Schools took to ethnography (see Burawoy 2000). Whether focused on the study of institutions, studying delimited contexts or moving beyond the borders of the nation-state, emphasising class relations or the functional integration of people into a wider society, ethnography's techniques have been responsive to changing times. However, often current conceptions of ethnography continue to derive from a positivist approach to social research, despite numerous works (see Van Maanen 1988; MacClancy 2002) that deconstruct the link between ethnography and exoticism for example. Earl Babbie for one still defines ethnography as typically referring to 'naturalistic observations and holistic understandings of cultures or subcultures' (1998:282). As Fay explains, holism methodologically typically 'offers a guide for theory construction in the social sciences: look to social wholes for bottom-line explanations' (1996:51). Instead of focusing on individual traits the individual is placed in larger systemic context that enables the formulation of explanatory theories of social phenomena through the holistic approach. John Lofland (1995:283) adds to this that analytic ethnographers proceed as if true realities exist, developing and using techniques that will accurately capture what is 'really' going on. The modernist orientation of such a stance is evident in the references to 'naturalistic observation (associated with an objective stance), 'wholeness', providing (as opposed to constructing) a 'truthful' account in the singular about individuals functioning within a larger system. Little wonder that Marit Melhuus (2002:79) believes the concept of holism is no longer plausible in a (postmodern) world in which 'boundaries are dissolved, people are displaced, identities are fragmented, concepts are dislocated...'

Ethnography is indeed still generally understood as a research method that can yield deeper, even 'intimate', understandings of the social and material conditions of contemporary phenomena. In its most traditional sense an ethnographer can help to 'translate' development plans to targeted beneficiaries, using their own 'cultural' idioms. So, for example, an ethnographic understanding of local conditions as opposed to standardised development 'solutions' might reduce the risk of false assumptions on the part of the project planners. An ethnographic sensitivity would entail making the premises and meaning of development terms such as 'community-building', 'sustainability' and 'participatory research' explicit. Local social dynamics would be examined, thereby ensuring among other things the appropriate timing of projects. As many role players as possible would be consulted by an ethnographer in an effort to establish their needs and priorities and monitor how such needs might change over time. A broader focus than economic indicators would be retained in order to determine the social impact of a project and project implementation and progress would be monitored on a continuous basis where possible. All of these ethnographic strategies can increase the achievement of development objectives both over the short and long run as actual case studies (see Chambers 1985; Gardner and Lewis 1996; De Waal 2002) have shown.

The qualitative data gathered by means of an ethnographic approach is often used in combination with quantitative data, since it is believed to enable the researcher to capture the subtle, symbolic processes that are not easily quantifiable. By linking the individual with the societal a more multifaceted analysis is constructed. A researcher studying poverty in a local context through participant observation and one-to-one interviews might, for example, show how lack of skills, resources and/or opportunities on the individual level are linked to institutionalised inequalities in terms of infrastructure, capital, land, education, information etc. In this regard ethnographers have been doing valuable work. The execution of social impact analyses (see Goldman 2000) is merely one example.

But unlike Babbie (1998) and Lofland (1995) I believe the method of ethnography, at least in some areas, has responded to the crisis of representation that started in the 1980s and that continues to haunt the social sciences today. The interrogation of the ethnographic method by postmodern scholars included allegations of cultural exploitation and a questioning of (researcher) authority. Postmodernists thus criticised ethnography as risking the imposition of 'ethnocentric, power-laden, analytic categories and exotifying images onto the unsuspecting people they study' (Bourgois 2002:19). Although widely contested by many, such accusations prompted a sensitisation to internal differentiation, neglected by a simplistic holism that conceives of groups as homogenous units; recognition of the narrative grounds of all knowledge claims; an unselfconscious foregrounding of the researcher's self and the generation of research that is open-ended, reflexive and multi-vocal and frequently challenges commonsense notions and taken-for-granted 'cultural' knowledge. Instead of the stereotypical referral to the ethnographer as 'gazing from another culture on practices' (Bohman 1991:204), contemporary ethnographers are situated in the betwixt and between spaces of societies. They are simultaneously on the margins and in the midst of social action as contexts shift and overlap.

Accounting for the fluidity of social relations, especially in Africa, has become paramount. Ethnographic analyses are thus able to account for diversity not just between different development contexts but also within the communities of professional developers and/or the 'targets' of such projects. Apart from these research strengths, it is likely that ethnographers who have been responsive to the postmodern turn nowadays share a commitment, or at least an awareness of, certain elements that are essential to the process of conducting and representing contemporary ethnographic research. These elements, of which I can explore only a few in this paper, include an attention to *context*; conducting research that is *people centred*; *framing the local within the global*; an *awareness of power discrepancies*; not shying away from *complexity*; *attention to discourse*; and an *openness to critique*.

Putting context into context: Although ethnographers historically have been granted privileged access to a diverse range of contexts, such contexts used to be quite narrowly defined as rural and far-flung. Apart from the fact that almost any space occupied by people—including cyberspace—can nowadays be the location of an ethnographic study, observers have become more aware that they help to produce the multiple features of the contexts in which they find themselves (Bohman 1991:103). Context, according to my own understanding of the term as applied to the practice of ethnography, has superseded the notion of holism. The idea that one can capture a whole 'culture', belief system or societal phenomenon and concurrently prescribe a development remedy is outdated. Instead, the importance of context is emphasised as the practice of 'paying close attention to particular practices and the setting(s) within which they are located' (Stern 2003:185), and combining historical and contemporaneous insights utilising a variety of traditions and approaches including historical documents and other textual sources. Context in a development discussion would therefore entail defining development in more than merely quantitative terms. Clashing concepts of development and divergent meanings attached to resources, for example, are capturing the attention of ethnographers (see Schneider 2002:69) who study the formation of land and labour markets in the heavily colonised regions of Africa.

People centred: Any unilaterally conceived position imposed by a political, civil, bureaucratic, or academic elite without some attempt to involve wider public opinion has in the experience of parts of Africa proved wasteful and ineffectual (Prah 1993:13). Ethnography has always been about taking people seriously (MacClancy 2002:4) through foregrounding what ordinary people say and do. Because of the reliance on informants, ethical guidelines for ethnographic research stipulate that research should empower research participants by respecting and protecting the rights of autonomy, dignity, privacy, and confidentiality. Increasingly, as an extension of the informed consent principle, the trend is towards making research participants worthy partners in research, instead of mere subjects. Ethnography is particularly suited for such collaboration since relations of trust are established over a prolonged period of time between the ethnographer and informants. However, as Taylor (1992:234) points out, there are many different variations on participation and it is crucial that the conditions under which community participation or development from below can emerge must be specified. Sandra Harding (2003:302) also warns that

> If research is to be accountable only to disciplinary conceptual frameworks and methodological requirements that in fact often service ruling institutions but not the 'ruled', more research will succeed in further entrenching such ruling conceptual frameworks and increasing the gap between the 'haves' and the 'have-nots'.

While making people participatory subjects 'endowed with intellectual capacities to contest and interrogate the purpose of their practice and to make autonomous and informed choices' (Letseka 1997:465) with regard to development is no foolproof strategy for empowerment, it serves to make development research more accountable to those who are supposed to benefit directly from it. As Bohman (2002:93) rightly points out the demand for criticism grounded in grand theory is increasingly rejected in favour of a more pluralistic approach in which 'criticism is verified by those participating in the practice'.

An ethnographic approach to development can also contribute to the validation of so-called indigenous knowledge. African resistance to imperialist ways of knowing imposed from 'outside' has led to a call for the greater appreciation of indigenous knowledge forms in which 'colonial and imperial imposition is absent' (George et al. 2000:7). Defined as a body of knowledge that has been 'accumulated by a group of people... who by centuries of unbroken residence develop an in-depth understanding of their particular place' (Roberts 1998:59 cited in George Sefa 2000:71), social researchers utilising ethnographic techni- ques, have succeeded in bringing to international attention that 'traditional' forms of knowledge and organisation have contributed to environmental sustainability in many localities (Leach and Fairhead 2002:209). The practice of ethnography, as a multidisciplinary research method, presents one with ways of offering a 'critical rereading of African and western theories and interpretations in order to expand the possibilities for knowledge production in the future' (Moore 1996:5). Ethnographers for example can foreground the meaning and behaviour of 'subjects' with regard to developmental practices (note the quotation marks), while simultaneously going beyond an interpretative approach confined to the 'schemes of meaning' (Fay 1996:127) operative in a given context by conducting a multi-level analysis that factors local knowledge into account. Moreover, while bottom-up approaches to development (as opposed to top-down, autocratic development policy) have become more popular since the 1990s, ethnographers are particularly well positioned to study both 'up' and 'down' by also interviewing elites in governing structures and examining organisational practices.

Situating the local within the global: What people typically can 'do' depends in part upon their locations in social structures (Harding 2003:296). One of the core advantages of a multi-level ethnographic analysis is that a consideration of macro factors that constrain development, such as certain agricultural policies of industrialised nations and/or the debt-servicing burden of African countries, can be integrated with a consideration of micro factors such as the gendered nature of labour, constraints on community/individual decision making, the local class structures, and differing access to resources and the physical environment. Gardner and Lewis (1996:18) stress that while it is important 'to analyse the structures which perpetuate under-development... we must also recognize individual agency in surviving under difficult conditions'. Specifically with regard to the exploration of development issues and local responses to difficult economic conditions, situating the local within the global becomes crucial as a means of approaching the heterogeneous responses to globalisation on the ground. While Henrietta Moore (1996:2) claims that one consequence of the 'the unravelling of grand narratives and totalising theories' with respect to the social sciences has been 'a call to specificity, to the local', James Peacock (2002:65) urges ethnographers to think and act both locally and globally. As always the conduct of research thus remains a careful balancing act between theory and action, policy and practice, engagement and disengagement, association and dissociation, specificity and comparison. I believe that thick description and the provision of a rich context should not be incommensurable with a comparative approach to the study of different development schemes across Africa. Unfortunately due to the length constraints of the paper I could not elaborate on the other elements of a critical ethnography such as an awareness of power discrepancies; not shying away from complexity; attention to discourse and openness to critique that I have mentioned at the outset of my discussion, although I have touched on these points implicitly. Novel developments in ethnographic writing such as experimenting with different narrative forms (see Van Maanen 1988) or using multiple levels and styles of analysis (see Marcus 1998) are evidence of the attempts to adapt the practice of ethnography to the postmodern demands of knowledge production. Although not equally successful I believe that some of these measures might enable ethnographers to better deal with African developmental concerns.

Conclusion

Social research is not always popular among policy planners because of social researchers' emphasis on the complexity, variability and indeterminacy of both the actual social phenomena and their own interpretations of it, which make them hesitant to offer concrete solutions. Nevertheless, Fay (1996:236) highlights three aspects of a critical social science that illustrates its usefulness for people: improving the possibilities for communication by making it possible for people to engage in dialogue; increasing self-knowledge through knowledge of others; and the enlargement of moral imagination by extending knowledge beyond the familiar. Framed like this, Fay's points echo the traditional conception of ethnography as a method that has the 'potential of mediating understanding and resolving essential points of cultural conflicts by explaining the occurrence of misunderstandings and providing... resolutions' (Chambers 1985:176). But as I have shown throughout this paper, all of these elements have been problematised to a degree. Instead of the ethnographer cast as cultural broker enabling dialogue between powerful organisations and passive subjects, local people are increasingly regarded as active research partners in development schemes, although the extent to which the practice fits the rhetoric varies. Moreover, the dialectic between self/other relations has been deconstructed as ethnographers do not only deal with culturally distant peoples, but also turn their gazes inward to consider their 'own' societies (see Marcus 1998). Nevertheless, certain traditional qualities of ethnography retain its value. One example is the insider-outsider dichotomy that highlights the importance of taking multiple perspectives into account when conducting developmental research: doing 'inside' research but simultaneously approaching the matter from 'behind', beneath', or 'outside', in order to obtain the distance deemed necessary for action-orientated social criticism. Thus ethnographers can contribute to developmental thought and practice, 'both by working in development and also by providing a critical account of development' as Gardner and Lewis (1996:25) suggest.

It is my contention that, although re-evaluating the production of knowledge is crucial, such an auto-critique should never overshadow the importance of developing conceptual frameworks for developmental research that are anti-essentialist, or the value of adhering to carefully constructed ethical codes. Research can be empowering for all the participants if one accepts James Bohman's (2003:92) suggestion that social science, by transforming reflexive social inquiry into practical knowledge, lets agents gain the sort of knowledge needed for effective social agency and freedom in the social world. I have chosen to focus on ethnography, because of my own familiarity with the research method and my firm believe that development should take into account local understandings and build on the ability of local peoples to generate and apply their own knowledges (George and Sefa 2000:80). Such an approach does not remove the problems surrounding selectivity, perspective, the making of assumptions, the exclusion of certain voices and so on, but it does leave scope for the consideration of multiple perspectives grounded in a fine-grained analysis that is carried out over a period of time. Retaining a comparative scope intra and between African countries is also crucial in order to prevent research fragmentation. Although paying attention to emerging development discourse between African governments, non-governmental organisations, funding agencies, locally based initiatives, focussing on what is emerging in action has always been central to development research conducted by ethnographers (see Grillo 1997). The postmodern turn has highlighted key issues that a flexible approach to development should be able to accommodate. While there are no unitary development theories or foolproof strategies, I do not believe that the search for empowerment through the expansion of possibilities for knowledge production about development is passé. Various social research methods such as survey research, content analysis and focus groups have proven that they can yield valuable insights on developmental issues when suitably applied. In this brief paper I am acutely aware of the little that I could address. I have not touched on the factors that discourage the adoption of an ethnographic approach to development (see Pottier 1993) and the examination of actual case studies fell beyond my scope.

In conclusion, it is essential that an action strategy for future research should foreground the promotion of research skills acquisition; rigorous theorising; explanatory frames that are simultaneously open-ended, flexible and adaptive to changing circumstances; the strengthening of academic and research communities; improving ways of disseminating research results; involving more social actors in research frameworks; generating research that is open to public scrutiny; revising criteria of adequacy and evaluation, and so on. Instead of viewing the indeterminacy of social phenomena as a stumbling block, I agree with Bohman (1991:13) that the recognition of indeterminacy, as foregrounded by postmodern thinking, does not exclude the possibility of 'constructing adequate and fruitful explanations that can fulfil a variety of purposes'. And it is here that ethnographers and social scientists in general are well positioned to provide such explanations.

Bibliography

Abrahams, J., 1997, 'Knowledge and Method', in J. Mouton and J. Muller, eds., *Knowledge, Method and the Public Good*, Pretoria: Human Sciences Research Council.

Babbie, E., 1998, *The Practice of Social Research*, Belmont: Wadsworth Publishing Company.

Bernard, H.R., 1988, *Research Methods in Cultural Anthropology*, Thousand Oaks, CA: Sage Publications.

Bohman, J., 1991, *New Philosophy of Social Science*, Oxford: Polity Press.

Bohman, J., 2003, 'Critical Theory as Practical Knowledge: Participants, Observers, and Critics', in Turner, S.P. and Roth, P.A., eds., *The Blackwell Guide to the Philosophy of the Social Sciences*, UK, USA, Australia and Germany: Blackwell Publishing.

Burawoy, M., 2000, 'Reaching for the Global', in Burawoy, M; et al., eds., *Global Ethnography: Forces, Connections, and Imaginations in a Postmodern World*, Berkeley: University of California Press.

Bourgois, P., 2002, 'Understanding Inner-City Poverty: Resistance and Self-Destruction under U.S. Apartheid', in MacClancy, J., ed., *Exotic No More: Anthropology on the Front Lines*, Chicago: University of Chicago Press.

Chambers, E., 1985, *Applied Anthropology: A Practical Guide*, Illinois: Waveland Press Inc.

Collier, M.J., 1998, 'Researching cultural identity: Reconciling Interpretive and Postcolonial Perspectives', in Tanno, D. & Gonzalez, A., eds., *Communication and Identity across Cultures*, Thousand Oaks, CA: Sage.

De Waal, A., 2002, 'Anthropology and the Aid Encounter', in *Exotic No More: Anthropology on the Front Lines*, MacClancy J. (ed.), Chicago, University of Chicago Press.

Fay, B., 1987, *Critical Social Science*, Ithaca: Cornell University Press.

Fay, B., 1996, *Contemporary Philosophy of Social Science: A Multicultural Approach*, UK: Blackwell Publishers.

Fruzzetti, L. and Ostor, A., 1990, *Culture and Change along the Blue Nile*, Boulder, San Francisco and London: Westview Press.

Gardner, K. and Lewis, D., 1996, *Anthropology, Development and the Postmodern Challenge*, London, Chicago, Illinois: Pluto Press.

George, J., et al., 2000, *Indigenous Knowledges in Global Contexts*, Toronto, Buffalo, London: University of Toronto Press.

George, J. and Sefa, Dei, 2000, 'African Development', in *Indigenous Knowledges in Global Contexts*, Toronto, Buffalo, London: University of Toronto Press.

Gingrich, A. and Fox, R.G., eds., 2002, *Anthropology, by Comparison*, London and New York: Routledge.

Goldman, L.R., ed., 2000, *Social Impact Analysis*, Oxford, New York: Berg.

Gordon, S., 1991, *The History and Philosophy of Social Science*, London and New York: Routledge.

Grillo, R.D., 1997, 'Discourses of Development: The View from Anthropology', in Grillo, R.D. and Stirrat, R. L., eds., *Discourses of Development: Anthropological Perspectives*, Oxford and New York: Berg.

Harding, S., 2003, 'How Standpoint Methodology Informs Philosophy of Social Science', in Turner, S.P. and Roth, P.A., eds., *The Blackwell Guide to the Philosophy of the Social Sciences*, UK, USA, Australia and Germany: Blackwell Publishing.

Independent Commission on Population and Quality of Life, 1996, *Caring for the Future*, New York: Oxford University Press.

International Research Network, http://www.childwatch.uio.no/ (19 September 2003).

Kellner, H., 2003, 'Literary Criticism: Social Science Between Fact and Figures', in Turner, S.P. and Roth, P.A., eds., *The Blackwell Guide to the Philosophy of the Social Sciences*, UK, USA, Australia and Germany: Blackwell Publishing.

Leach, M. and Fairhead, J., 2002, 'Anthropology, Culture, and Environment', in MacClancy, J. ed., *Exotic No More: Anthropology on the Front Lines*, Chicago: University of Chicago Press.

Letseka, M., 1997, 'Research and the Empowerment of Teachers', *Knowledge and Method*, Pretoria: Human Sciences Research Council.

Lofland, J., 1995, 'Analytic Ethnography: Features, Failings, and Futures', *Journal of Contemporary Ethnography*, 24 (1): 30-67.

MacClancy, J., ed., 2002, *Exotic No More: Anthropology on the Front Lines*,Chicago: University of Chicago Press.

Mackenzie, F., 1992, 'Development from Within? The Struggle to Survive', in D.R.F. and Mackenzie, F., eds., *Development from Within: Survival in Rural Africa*, London and New York: Routledge.

Marcus, G.E., 1998, *Ethnography Through Thick and Thin*, Princeton: Princeton University Press.

Melhuus, M., 2002, 'Issues of Relevance', in *Anthropology by Comparison*, London and New York: Routledge.

Messer, E. and Shipton, P., 2002, 'Hunger in Africa: Untangling its Human Roots', in MacClancy, J., ed., *Exotic No More: Anthropology on the Front Lines*, Chicago: University of Chicago Press.

Moore, H.L., ed., 1996, *The Future of Anthropological Knowledge*, London and New York: Routledge.

Mouton, J. and Muller, J., eds., 1997, *Knowledge, Method and the Public Good*, Pretoria: Human Sciences Research Council.

Peacock, J., 2002, 'Action Comparison: Efforts towards a Global and Comparative yet Local and Active Anthropology', in *Anthropology by Comparison*, London and New York: Routledge.

Pottier, J., ed., 1993, *Practicing Development: Social Science Perspectives*, London and New York: Routledge.

Prah, K.K., 1993, *Social Science Research Priorities for Namibia*, Eppingindust: University of Namibia and the Council for the Development of Economic and Social Research in Africa.

Schneider, J., 2002, 'World Markets: Anthropological Perspectives', in MacClancy, J., ed., *Exotic No More: Anthropology on the Front Lines*, Chicago: University of Chicago Press.

Stern, D.G., 2003, 'The Practical Turn', in Turner, S.P. and Roth, P.A., eds., *The Blackwell Guide to the Philosophy of the Social Sciences*, Oxford UK, Cambridge USA, Australia and Germany: Blackwell Publishing.

Taylor, D.R.F., 1992, 'Development from Within and Survival in Rural Africa: A Synthesis of Theory and Practice', in Taylor, D.R.F. and Mackenzie, F., eds., *Development from Within*, London and New York: Routledge.

Turner, S.P. and Roth, P.A., 2003, 'Ghosts and the Machine: Issues of Agency, Rationality, and Scientific Methodology in Contemporary Philosophy of Social Science', in Turner, S.P. and Roth, P.A., eds., *The Blackwell Guide to the Philosophy of the Social Sciences*, UK, USA, Australia and

Germany: Blackwell Publishing.

Turner, T., 1994, 'Anthropology and Multiculturalism: What Is Anthropology that Multiculturalists Should be Mindful of It?', in Goldberg, D.T., ed., *Multiculturalism: A Critical Reader*, Oxford UK and Cambridge USA: Blackwell.

Van Maanen, J., 1988, *Tales of the Field*, Chicago: University of Chicago Press.

Wangoola, P., 2000, 'Global Ethnography', in Burawoy, M., et al., eds., *Global Ethnography* Berkeley, Los Angeles, London: University of California Press.

Wicker, H.R., 1997, 'From Complex Culture to Cultural Complexity', *Debating Cultural Hybridity*.

Liberation or Oppression? Social Sciences, Politics and the Postcolonial Context

Ingrid Palmary

Introduction

People from Kenya are smiling
People from Zaire are smiling
Because discrimination has been conquered
You have enslaved me apartheid
For you said anthropology makes into slaves
Yet anthropology liberates people
You have discriminated against me apartheid
For you said anthropology discriminates
Yet anthropology unites peoples
You have driven me backwards apartheid
For you said anthropology moves backward
Yet anthropology makes people advance[1]

This paper will consider the role that the social sciences have played in the political, economic and social development of the African continent. Like the words of the praise poet above, this article reflects the mixed and sometimes contradictory views on the value of the social sciences for Africa. I would, however, add that the ambivalent words of the praise poet, far from being exclusive to anthropology, can be extended to all the social sciences including development studies, sociology and psychology. In order to consider the necessity and relevance of the social sciences for the future one needs to consider the social value that they have. I will argue that the social sciences have been central to Africa's liberation from colonialism and its continuing struggle against oppression, conflict and economic inequality. This is a role that the social sciences can continue to play through critical engagement with the political structures and systems emerging out of Africa's ongoing democratisation and increasing distance from its colonial past. I will also argue, however, that the social sciences have been central to the development of racist and other oppressive practices on the African continent. This is already fairly well documented; however, what is less well acknowledged is that, far from being a phenomenon of a colonial past, social science continues to produce social research and theory that furthers racist, sexist and other oppressive practices. I argue that this outcome is, at least in part, a result of the failure of social researchers and theorists to anticipate and engage critically with the political environment in which their research is produced and re-produced and how patterns of continuity and change in systems of domination are emerging on the continent.

In this sense, social science is a powerful tool that often implicitly, but occasionally quite explicitly, remains a medium for the justification of continued inequality. I will argue this point by considering a short case study of xenophobia in South Africa. This example will illustrate my argument that without a critically reflexive and politically engaged social science we risk justifying new expressions of oppression. I have chosen this example because it highlights how a failure to recognise that new forms of prejudice are emerging in South Africa (and indeed across the continent) which cannot be easily understood within the traditional binaries of colonisation (black/white; male/female) can leave scientific racism unchecked. It also highlights the difficulty that many social scientists face in producing a useful and relevant practice and how difficult it is to predict the use to which social research will be put, in advance. The relationship between social research, social theory, policy and popular perceptions is complex. It is seldom (probably never) causal with one feeding neatly into the other and we cannot very easily anticipate how our research and theory will be used. For the social sciences to be necessary for the future this complexity needs to be grappled with more explicitly and we need to be able to adapt to, learn from, and influence popular discourses and policy.

Thus it is my contention that the necessity of the social sciences depends on the political use to which they are put and the possibilities of developing a social science that can engage with both continuing practices of social inequality and oppression as well as changing patterns of marginalisation as they manifest themselves across the continent. This contention requires explanation because social science cannot automatically be assumed to be a force of progress, 'development' and greater equality in Africa. It has a history of being useful for both oppressive and liberatory ends and, as I shall explain, it is not always clear from the outset which end it will ultimately serve. Indeed the intentions and political positioning of the social scientist are often subverted in the way in which her research is taken up as the case study below shall show.

Social Science: A practice of liberation?

For development to be meaningful, it would appear on the surface as if social research and public policy must not be too far apart; that the one must borrow from the other. One probably cannot do without the other and they must be considered as two sides of the same coin (Olurode 1998).

Can the social sciences be a practice of liberation that will render them necessary to African recovery from the colonial era? Or, perhaps as importantly, have they already played this role in the past? Several authors have argued that, far from simply being colonial artefacts, the social sciences have and continue to make a contribution in Africa and are, therefore, necessary for the post-colonial continent (see for example, Guyer 1999). Indeed, Vilikazi (2001) goes so far as to suggest that it is the duty of social scientists to play this role:

> We African intellectuals are wrong on blaming individual
> African leaders of State for failing to move Africa forward
> when we ourselves have not done our pre-requisite duty,
> namely, to formulate, debate and publicise, a compelling,
> Africa-centred, development paradigm, which these leaders
> can use to move the continent forward (p. 75).

He goes on to argue for the extension of social research so that this new development paradigm can emerge. Clearly this is a view that sees the potential for the social sciences to rid the African context of its history of poverty and injustice— even if we have fallen short of this task on many occasions.

If we consider the history of African scholarship, it is clear that there are times when the social sciences have played a meaningful role in struggles for equity, particularly anti-colonial struggles across the continent. Speaking of the intellectuals of the 1950s and 1960s, Vilikazi (2001) states that 'this community sought to change the world, not only in practice, but in thought, too. We believed very strongly that the changing of the world, in practice, must go hand in hand with the changing of the world of thought' (p. 75). This was not unique to this time. As early as 1953, when Africa was still emerged in colonial conquests, Myrdal stated that 'the social sciences have all received their impetus much more from the urge to improve society than from simple curiosity about its working' (cited in Uchendu 1978 p. 7). Thus, even at the height of colonisation there is evidence of a body of social research that was committed to greater equality and emancipation. Indeed, Uchendu (1978) sees the social sciences as key to undoing the effects of colonisation, and information as one of the defining features of modern societies. Olurode (1998) too argues that 'for social science to be relevant [however] there is an urgent need for the practitioners of the profession to be involved in the actual struggle to bring about concrete and sustainable democratic change' (p. 138). Similarly (and more recently) Nuttall and Michael stated that '... those engaged with an emergent Cultural Studies [and] with a transforming Social Sciences and Humanities in general, contribute to the building of a culture of democracy in the new nation' (1999:55).

Indeed the potential of the social sciences to cause radical shifts in our conceptualisation of the world has been evidenced in the ways in which those in power have often sought to regulate them. Olurode (1998) documents how in 1978, in Nigeria, lecturers were banned by the then military government from discussing politics and again in 1985 were warned against using lectures for 'anti-social' activities, which it interprets as the teaching of radical ideas. The targeting of universities and other centres of learning because of their potential to challenge the status quo has been equally common in other countries and is indicative of the relationship, however complex, between social theory, research and social change.

Similarly, few could rival Frantz Fanon's exposition of colonial violence or his engagement with the emerging revolution in Africa. It is difficult to dismiss such writing as irrelevant or unnecessary. Indeed, Dane (1994) states that 'Fanon is effective in at least six roles: political biographer, political philosopher, social scientist, revolutionary theorist, utopian and voice for ethical reform' (p. 72). This hints at a challenge posed to all social scientists grappling research in post-colonial Africa which will be considered in more detail later on. That is, for the discipline to be relevant to current concerns in post-colonial Africa it requires, at least, a significant cross disciplinary and multi-faceted approach and, at most, a rejection of current methods and concepts altogether.

In addition, the social sciences have been used to challenge prevailing prejudices that have extended beyond specific colonial projects. Few could argue that the feminist/women's movement in Africa, which like in other contexts has been rooted in the relationship between research, critical theory, activism and politics, has not had a positive effect on African women. For example, feminists have challenged the role that emerging African nationalisms have played in legitimating the violent control over women's bodies as witnessed in the use of rape as a strategy of war and the symbolic destruction of women's reproductive systems (Malkki 1995). They have highlighted the ways in which control of reproduction has been central for nationalist and colonial projects and challenged the representation of African women as politically passive by both colonial and post-colonial powers (Fenster 1998; Mama 2001).

We also see in the literature the extent to which methodology is implicated in these debates. Mafeje (1998) notes how research from the South has been useful for its attack on European ethnocentrism and the movement for the development of a more indigenous social science both in concept and methodology. This is not unlike the challenges posed by Southern women to Western feminism and its essentialising statements about 'women's interests' which have hegemonised the developing world (Pearson and Jackson 1998;

Cook and Kothari 2001). Similarly, feminism's challenges to nationalism have reminded us that romantic images of a pre-colonial time have been no less violent in their scripting of identity than colonial powers that practice(d) domination in the name of development. Thus, although the above examples show that the social sciences have always had a role to play in macro-level anti-colonial struggles as well as more micro-level struggles, there is extreme dissatisfaction in the post-colonial literature and it is becoming clear that significant changes are needed for the social sciences to remain relevant to African needs (see Mafeje 1998; Cook and Kothari 2001; Mohanty 1991). Some writers have argued that the social sciences in Africa are essential to self-liberation and self-knowledge whilst others dismiss them entirely as inherently racist and Anti-African.

Ndebele (cited in Nuttal and Michael 1999) argued for the importance of a history from below which would require us to re-consider what we accept as knowledge and would give increasing recognition to popular forms of knowledge. Nuttal and Michael (1999) argue that since the beginning of democracy in South Africa, around 1991, there has been an increasingly fluid space between the work of the universities and the work of the print media. In addition, new disciplines such as cultural studies which focus on the study of marginalised identities have emerged. These authors illustrate the extent to which the social context in which we work can, at least in part, influence the extent to which our work can be considered radical. Further challenges to the institutions of the social sciences have included the increasing research undertaken by NGOs which have, in some cases, resulted in increasing the relationship between research and activism.

Each of these criticisms is complex and subject to ongoing debate. As our practice develops in the post-colonial era, so new forms of discrimination, inequality and oppression emerge—and indeed are justified by research claiming to be radically different from colonial research. Thus the challenge has become how to subvert the crass and fixed notions of identity central to colonial projects and re-think the ways in which race, ethnicity and gender work in the post-colonial context. Indeed, for the social sciences to remain relevant for the future, these debates are perhaps one of the most important activities we can engage in. Therefore, I will consider them in more detail in the section that follows.

Social Science: A Practice of Oppression?

Traditionally the social sciences have been a tool for the measurement of difference, particularly in their more quantitative form. As such they have developed systems of classifying and coding the world (see for example Bless and Kathuria 1993). These classifications and divisions have been taken to be objective observations of existing social categories, a belief which undermined critical reflection on the possible role that research may play in co-constructing such social chasms. However, more recently this notion of a social science that observes and documents the world has been challenged. It has been convincingly argued that far from simply describing the world, the social sciences, construct, create and impose difference, and that the kinds of constructions that emerge from social science research cannot be understood outside of the social and political context in which we work. It is the positioning of the social scientists in their political and social reality which influences their account of the world. For example, Mamdani (2001) in his research into the conflict in the Great Lakes region indicates how one of the first pieces of colonial social research in the region showed that Tutsis were nearly ten centimetres taller than Hutus. He goes on to illustrate how it was these early forms of research that were used to imply historical and ethnic difference between the two groups. Although there is some debate about whether notions of Hutu and Tutsi existed prior to colonisation, it is clear that the political status of these identities was shaped and given political-historical meaning by colonial social science research (Mamdani 2001). Thus, the social sciences were used to legitimate practices of inequality and exclusion which served the ultimate interests of the colonisers. Far from being limited to this extreme example, the social categorisation and documentation of social categories can never be politically neutral. The categories that we find are shaped by what we expect to find, our current understandings of the world and the particular purpose for which they are documented.

Not only have the social sciences classified the world in ways that facilitated colonial rule, they have also failed to challenge the racial, sexual and nationalist classifications that have been developed through popular movements and discourse. Through the anthropological field notes and sociological interviews, mythical-historical social identities have been uncritically restated as fact. For example, in the 1940s, apartheid policy makers were easily able to draw on development studies as an emerging field of social research because of its perpetuation of racial constructs. In this way, development studies became useful to justify forced removals of black Africans from their land and for forms of racial segregation. It also stepped in at a time when popularly expressed theories of racial superiority were attracting critique and in this way it provided apartheid planners with a politically correct language and a seemingly logical and research-based justification for continuing policies of 'separate development' (Tapscott 1995). Statistics were produced to show that while white South Africans lived a first world status, black South Africans lived a third world status. As a result, the stated aims of 'separate development' were to 'develop different peoples of whom many are still at the beginning of the long road towards democracy and economic and technological self-management' (Bantu Investment Corporation 1975:11, cited in Tapscott 1995). Far from being a uniquely prejudiced discipline, anthropology, psychology and other related disciplines were also drawn on as evidence of the traditionalism of African society to further legitimate such practices. Thus by assuming apartheid racial classifications to be accurate without reflecting on their historical and social production, social science research could be used to justify political and economic oppression in the name of 'respect for culture'.

It is, of course, too easy with hindsight to critically examine the role of the social sciences in furthering the project of colonisation and apartheid in Africa. This leaves unquestioned the more subtle, unintentional and less visible ways in which the social sciences have been implicated in reinforcing social divisions and inequalities as well as the ways in which some African scholars have perpetuated this approach to social research. For example, Mohanty (1991) laments that when studying gender relations in Africa, 'third world women' have often appropriated the methods and conclusions of colonial researchers (Mohanty 1991). Similarly, in Africa and internationally, women have sometimes been at the forefront of fundamentalist movements which have marginalised other groups of women (Sahgal and Yuval-Davis 1990). Also, research claiming to be feminist has reproduced, in some cases, sexist notions of women as weak and entirely powerless by looking for evidence in specific contexts and then generalising it to all women (Mohanty 1991). Thus to assume that it is sufficient for social science to simply be conducted from Africa or by Africans is insufficient to meaningfully challenge systems of inequality on the continent. In this context, much African feminism has been useful in highlighting the need to concentrate on how 'African' interests are formed, by whom and in what context (Molyneux 1998). Far from undermining the oppressive nature of the social sciences often what has emerged are superficial changes which result in new forms of essentialism (i.e. the assumption that all African women are the same) rather than a critique of the history of our systems of classification. It is this dangerous mistake which makes it possible for Dr. Buthelezi, the then South African Minister of Home Affairs and leader of the Inkatha Freedom Party to say, in 1999, that 'separate development' is not necessarily a problem provided it is not imposed by Europeans.

> In fact, we are all Africans, daughters and sons of Africa. I strongly feel that the Afrikaners are a truly indigenous African nation. Therefore, our discussion on self-determination must find its own African parameters and must move away from preconceived European notions. I am convinced that if we undertake this exercise we may discover how the notion of self-determination can enrich the unity of South Africa rather than undermining it (Buthelezi 1999).

In the context of Afrikaner nationalism, self-determination often refers to the creation of a separate Afrikaner 'state' or area although it also extends to possible self-governance—Author's note.

This statement is surprisingly similar to the kinds of statements issued under apartheid which justified the original system of 'separate development'. In this way, rather than critiquing the very basis for our establishment of social groups, they are taken to be natural and already constituted, which makes room for further acts of oppression (see also Manzo 1998). Only by critiquing such ideas, can we begin to see how the rural women's movement in South Africa could be one of the organisations leading the campaign to limit the powers of traditional leaders. It is vital if the social sciences are to remain relevant to post-colonial Africa that we begin to recognise the multiple positions of people and consider how we can begin to subvert (and not simply invert) colonial social categories whilst at the same time considering how patterns of prejudice are continuous with and rooted in those of the past.

It has already been implied that even those with the most progressive intentions have—in another time and political context—been criticised for the ways in which their research has reinforced oppressive practices. Participatory Action Research (PAR) in the field of development studies has such a history. Participatory approaches to development were initially advocated as a solution to top-down approaches to development. It was hoped that they would increase beneficiary involvement and the decision making powers of the most marginal (Cooke and Kothari 2001). However, largely because these have been based on romanticised notions of community which assumed consensus and homogeneity, they have often served to reinforce the interests of already powerful members of that community (Gaujit and Kaul 1998). As Cleaver (2001) states, locally produced knowledge reflects local power. Again we see how a failure to critically reflect on the social categories that are taken for granted, even at a very local level, can reinforce these social divisions and further entrench them.

Similarly, across the continent, anti-colonial struggles have been fought on the basis of nationalism. This took the nation state to be an already constituted entity rather than a colonial imposition. It is expected then that nationalism will justify new practices of inequality. The case study below will describe how this has resulted in new systems of exclusion and oppression for those not belonging to a nation-state—such as displaced persons.

Finally, it is important to note that even the interventions that have been made on the basis of progressive social science have very often failed to meaningfully change forms of oppression that have persisted. For example, increasing access by women to the labour market, far from being liberating, at times, has increased, particularly in Southern countries, women's workload and has kept them exploited in poorly paid jobs (Pearson and Jackson 1998). Thus we need to celebrate change cautiously and examine more critically the political changes that have taken place. For example, one of the most important issues for social scientists will be ongoing monitoring of the status of women in Rwanda given that since the recent elections women hold 50 percent of the seats in the lower house and 30 percent in the upper house. An analysis of how sexism continues in the face of a gender representative parliament as well as the new forms it takes will need ongoing reflection and debate among academics and social researchers.

The Oppressive and Liberating Components of Current Day Social Science

Thus far, the examples drawn on have been purposefully diverse. I have attempted to show that although the social sciences have been necessary for the promotion of greater equality in post-colonial Africa and in the struggle against colonisation (and apartheid), continuing patterns of oppression and marginalisation persist albeit in new and mutating forms. The social sciences have been no less implicated in these developments as they were in the establishment of colonisation. The challenges made by the social sciences and the relationship between the social sciences and social movements have been complex and the use of the social sciences to justify acts of oppression continues in both its unintentional forms and its most overt ones. The example below is intended to give a present day illustration of how the complexities highlighted above continue to plague the social sciences in their engagement with social change of all kinds. It is purposefully specific given the broad and generalised examples referred to thus far.

Case Study of Xenophobia in South Africa

Much research has indicated that South Africans popularly believe that foreigners come to South Africa seeking better employment opportunities because of its wealth relative to the rest of the continent, (HSRC and ISS 1996; Harris 2001). There has also been a popular conflation of perceived increasing crime rates, unemployment and recent (post-1994) immigration to South Africa (Crush and Williams 2003; Palmary 2002). This is a very complex set of statements which needs to be unpacked in relation to the information we have on migration, crime and economic opportunity. This I will do by looking at the relationship between social research and popular understandings of migration in Southern Africa.

In the mid 1990s, the Human Sciences Research Council (HSRC) released a report which, among other things, stated that South Africa had between 2.4 and 4 million undocumented migrants in the country at any one time. This report has been widely cited (and indeed often exaggerated) particularly by the police who have used it to legitimate repressive policing practices such as 'Operation Crackdown' where large numbers of people are arrested on suspicion of being in the country illegally. This is widely published in local newspapers as a crime prevention activity, as the following two short extracts illustrate:

> A total of 31 suspected illegal immigrants were arrested during the raids and drugs worth R70 000 were seized (*The Star*, 6 February 2002).

> A further 26 stolen vehicles valued at R680 000, 271kg of copper cable and dagga with a street value of more than R46 000 were also seized. Of those arrested, 391 were illegal immigrants' (SAPA 26 May 2000).

Research with the Johannesburg metropolitan police department indicates that 30 percent of officers believed crime to be caused by foreigners (Palmary 2002). The assumption that crime in South Africa is caused predominantly by 'illegal immigrants' has been perpetuated at the highest levels of government and indeed by the very department required to manage migration. This belief that foreigners (most of whom are assumed to be illegally in the country) are responsible for crime is largely based on the assumption that other Africans are poorer than South Africans and are therefore more likely to turn to crime.

This report has since been publicly withdrawn by the HSRC from where it originated (Orkin 2002 cited in Crush and Williams 2001; *HSRC Review* 2003). In spite of this, it has continued to be used. In response to the continued use of these figures in spite of their withdrawal, in 2003, the HSRC stated once more that the study had been withdrawn, primarily because the methodology used had resulted in greatly overestimated figures (*HSRC Review* 2003). The methodology used was to ask South Africans how many illegal immigrants lived nearby them. This does not account for different families identifying the same 'illegal immigrants' or for the likelihood that few South Africans know the difference between categories of migrants and tend to consider all foreigners to be illegal immigrants. In addition to the acknowledgement that this research was based on flawed methodology, the vast majority of social research on migration in South Africa does not support this view of widespread illegal immigration and its link to high crime. Research undertaken by Lawyers for Human Rights at the Lindela repatriation centre outside Johannesburg showed that one-fifth of those in Lindela deportation centre were in fact South Africans who had not been given the opportunity to show their identity documents (Human Rights Watch 1998). Thus the large numbers of arrest of undocumented migrants are likely to be based simply on indiscriminate arrests of all people who do not 'look' South

African. In addition, in spite of statements by the South African Police Services that illegal immigrants are widely involved in crime, their own statistics indicate that between 81 percent and 99 percent of all crime in South Africa was perpetrated by South Africans, depending on the nature of the crime (CIAS 1998). Similarly, research by the Southern African Migration Project indicates that far from people migrating to South Africa to find employment, patterns of migration across Southern Africa are circular, often based on informal trade across countries and seldom result in paid employment (Crush and Williams 2003). In spite of the vast majority of research therefore contradicting statements in the media, by the Department of Home Affairs and the various policing services, none of this research has been picked up, and the now infamous HSRC report continues to be cited— much to the frustration of social scientists working for the rights of migrant groups (especially those from the HSRC).

In addition to a very selective use of research, there are times where statistics and other 'objective' research findings are cited with no clear indication of where they come from or whether there is indeed any research backing up these claims. For example, The ANC's ex-director of Home Affairs stated in 2002 that 'approximately 90 percent of foreign persons who are in RSA with fraudulent documents, i.e., either citizenship or migration documents, are involved in other crimes as well... it is quicker to charge these criminals for their false documentation and then to deport them than to pursue the long route in respect of the other crimes that are committed' (cited in Crush and Williams 2003).

Discussion

The example highlights the complexity of establishing the necessity of the social sciences in Africa. It reflects the debate on their oppressive potential in several ways. Firstly, it provides

an illustration of how social research very often does not find
its way into public policy and popular perceptions. When it
does, it is often because it suits the intentions of those that
use it, rather than because it is credible or good quality
research. Crush's statement that power decides what becomes
knowledge and what does not, becomes relevant here (Crush
1995). Similarly, research produced in the mid 1990s has found
renewed popularity because of the changing political context.
That is, a report produced in the 1990s has become popular
only recently because of the social function that it can perform,
that is, to legitimate repressive policing that targets
undocumented migrants.

Similarly, there has been a lack of analysis of how current
xenophobia in South Africa is both a continuation of
apartheid-constructed social categories as well as a new
emerging form of prejudice for South Africa. In other words,
expressions of xenophobia draw heavily from apartheid social
stratifications. Anecdotal evidence suggests that when police
were asked how they recognise 'illegal immigrants' the most
common way was because they were darker skinned than most
South Africans. In addition, tests such as asking a person to
speak a local language are often used as indicators of a person's
right to be in the country. Thus the apartheid categories which
graded people according to skin colour continue to be used
and adapted to new situations. However, there are clear
differences in the way in which xenophobia manifests itself.
Perhaps the most striking difference is that black and white
South Africans alike see foreigners as a threat. Thus it is
possible that new systems of social categorisation are again
being used to uphold the status quo (that is the perceived
relative wealth of South Africa compared to other African
countries). There is little discursive room for this kind of
analysis in South Africa because of the salience of racial
categories and the lack of analytic tools to consider how black

and white South Africans could express xenophobic sentiments which in other contexts have themselves been called racism.

The response of the social scientists to this kind of (mis)use of research has been noble but largely ineffective. Some of the research that contradicts theories of mass immigration has been outlined above. However, none of this has been cited to the extent of the HSRC report and there have been few spaces where social scientists and academics have challenged these stereotypes in public forums. This paralysis is possibly the biggest threat to the relevance of the social sciences. If we are unable to interject into public debates, then it is likely that social science will simply continue to be used for repressive ends. Also, very little criticism of the nation-state and the historical production of African borders through the colonial project has emerged. Thus, as is described above, the social categorisation on which prejudice is based remains unchallenged.

This also speaks to the importance of social scientists in Africa being engaged with emerging social movements and reflecting critically on the ways in which social science is being taken up by such movements. These relationships are far from simple but need to be at the forefront of a useful, relevant and necessary social science.

Conclusion

I have argued that the necessity of the social sciences needs to be evaluated in terms of their ability to challenge the forms of discrimination and oppression which are both rooted in colonisation and at the same time finding new and resilient forms of expression.

The social sciences are both a tool for supporting such inequality and for challenging it. Thus it is central that research be critically reflected on in relation to the political, social and historical context in which it is being produced and the interests that it serves. In such a context it can be a necessary tool for the dismantling of the institutions of colonisation. In other words, social science cannot be celebrated as necessary or rejected as unnecessary without an analysis of the context in which it is produced and the ways in which it is used. This remains the central task of social scientists.

Note

1. Extract from a praise poem presented at the Joint Conference of the Pan African Anthropological Association and the Association for Anthropology in Southern Africa, Pretoria, South Africa.

References

Bless, C., and Kathuria, R., 1993, *Fundamentals of Social Statistics: An African Perspective*, Cape Town: Juta.

Buthelezi, M., 1999, Speech during the International Conference on Self-Determination Organised by the Afrikaner Volkstaat Council.

CIAS, 1998, 'The Nationality of Arrestees', Pretoria.

Cook, B., and Kothari, U., 2001, 'The Case for Participation as Tyranny', in B. Cooke, and U. Kothari, eds., *Participation the New Tyranny*, London: Zed Books.

Crush, J. and Williams, V., 2001, 'Making up the Numbers: Measuring "illegal immigration" to South Africa', *Migration Policy Brief*, 3, Southern African Migration Project.

Crush J., and Williams, V., 2003, 'Criminal Tendencies: Immigrants and Illegality in South Africa', *Migration Policy Brief*, 10, Southern African Migration Project.

Dane, R., 1994, 'When Mirror Turns Lamp: Frantz Fanon as Cultural Visionary', *Africa Today*, 41(2): 70-92.

Fenster, T., 1989, 'Ethnicity, Citizenship, Planning and Gender: The Case of the Ethiopian Women in Israel', *Gender, Place and Culture*, 5(2): 177-189.

Gaujit I., and Kaul, K. S., 1998, *The Myth of Community: Gender Issues in Participatory Development*, London: Intermediate Technology Productions.

Guyer, J., 1999, 'Anthropology: The Study of Social and Cultural Originality', *African Sociological Review*, 3(2): 30-53.

Harris, B., 2001, *A Foreign Experience: Violence, Crime and Xenophobia during South Africa's Transition*, Violence and Transition Series, Johannesburg, CSVR [Available online: http://www.csvr.org.za].

Human Sciences Research Council (HSRC) and Institute for Security Studies (ISS), 1996, 'Consolidated Results of a Nation-wide Opinion Survey on Attitudes to Selected Security Issues', Pretoria.

HSRC Review, 2003, 'Figures on Illegal Immigrants Invalid', *HSRC Review*, 1(2), available online: http://www.hsrc.ac.za.

Human Rights Watch, 1998, 'Prohibited Persons: Abuse of Undocumented Migrants, Asylum Seekers and Refugees in South Africa', New York.

Mafeje, A., 1998, 'Anthropology and Independent Africans: Suicide or End of an Era', *African Sociological Review*, 2(1): 1-43.

Malkki, L. H., 1995, *Purity and Exile: Violence, Memory and National Cosmology among Hutu Refugees in Tanzania*, London: University of Chicago Press.

Mohanty, C. T., Russo, A., and Torres, L., 1991, *Third World Women and the Politics of Feminism*, Bloomington: Indiana University Press.

Mama, A., 2001, 'Challenging Subjects: Gender and Power in African Contexts', *African Sociological Review*, 5(2): 63-73.

Mamdani, M., 2001, *When Victims Become Killers: Colonialism, Nativism and the Genocide in Rwanda*, Princeton: Princeton University Press.

Manzo, K., 1998, 'Black Consciousness and the Quest for a Counter-modernist Development', in J. Crush ed., *The Power of Development*, London: Routledge.

Nuttall, S., and Michael, C., 1999, 'Re-imagining South African Cultural Studies', *African Sociological Review*, 3(2): 54-68.

Olurode, L., 1998, 'Social Research and Public Policy in Nigeria', *African Sociological Review*, 2(1): 136-152.

Palmary, I., 2002, *A Training Needs Assessment of Johannesburg Metropolitan Police Department*, Johannesburg, Unpublished Report.

Pearson R., and Jackson, C., 1998, 'Interrogating Development: Feminism, Gender and Policy', in R. Pearson and C. Jackson, eds., *Feminist Visions of Development*, London: Routledge.

Sahgal, G., and Yuval-Davis, N., 1990, 'Refusing Holy Orders', *Women Against Fundamentalism*, 1: 3-5.

SAPA, May 26 2000, '2000 Arrested in 'Operation Crackdown', Independent Online.

Tapscott, C., 1995, 'Changing Discourses of Development in South Africa', in J. Crush, ed., *The Power of Development*, London: Routledge.

The Star, February 6, 2002, "Police Raid Four 'Drug Havens' in Hillbrow", Independent Online.

Uchendu, V. C., 1978, 'The Applications of African Studies', in P. Stevens, ed., *The Social Sciences and African Development Planning*, Massachusetts: African Studies Association.

Vilikazi, H., 2001, 'African Intellectuals and the African Crisis: In Honour of Professor Ben Magubane', *African Sociological Review*, 5(2): 74-85.

www.ingramcontent.com/pod-product-compliance
Lightning Source LLC
Chambersburg PA
CBHW020239290326
41929CB00044B/342